INVINCIBI

Invincible Thinking

Ryuho Okawa

Lantern Books ● New York
A Division of Booklight Inc.

Lantern Books

A Division of Booklight Inc.

Lantern Books

128 Second Place

Brooklyn, NY 11231

www.lanternbooks.com

Library of Congress Cataloging-in-Publication Data

Okawa, Ryuho, 1956–

[Josho-Shikou. English]

Invincible thinking : there is no such thing as defeat / Ryuho Okawa.

p. cm.

ISBN 1-59056-051-5 (alk paper)

1. Kofuku no Kagaku (Organization)—Doctrines. 2. Conduct of life.

3. Success. I. Title.

BP605.K55O324513 2003

299'.93—dc21

2003011727

ISBN-13: 978-1-59056-051-8

Table of Contents

Postscript
About the Author
Lantern Books by Ryuho Okawa
What Is Happy Science?
Contacts

Preface to the New Edition

This book, written in an easy-to-understand way, gives us clues about how to succeed in life. Since it was first published in 1989, it has sold in excess of two million copies in Japan, and has became a favorite among leaders in every field, including politicians and corporate managers. It has also appeared in translation, allowing readers throughout the world to appreciate its ideas. Happy Science, which I founded, is the largest religion in Japan and continues to grow, taking its place among the major religions of the world.

However, at this time many countries are becoming increasingly disorganized both politically and economically, causing great unease among their peoples. For this reason, I wish to spread the message of this book, which teaches there is no such thing as defeat, imbuing people with courage and hope.

The aim of this book is to enable readers to become outstanding leaders, capable of showing others the right path. Invincible thinking is a philosophy that allows people to succeed in any situation. It is a methodology that makes it possible to find lessons in both success and failure, thus encouraging the development of leadership. It is a method of shaping your future in all weathers, using a combination of positive thinking and self-reflection.

Ryuho Okawa
President
Happy Science

Preface

Invincible thinking is a philosophy containing the power to achieve true victory in life. I have absolutely no intention of preaching some tawdry method of achieving success. In this book, I present a philosophy that is relevant to everyone, regardless of sex, age or nationality. No matter whether you are young or old, a man or woman, no matter what your nationality, if you pick this book up and read it to its conclusion, I can guarantee that you will clearly visualize a path to success opening up before you.

Life can be compared to a tunnel that is being drilled through a mountain; you may come across obstacles created by water or hard rock. However, here you have invincible thinking, which provides the dynamite to blast through solid rock, a drill to bore through all the barriers until you achieve your goals.

If you study this book and savor it, making its philos-

ophy your own strength, you will be able to declare
proudly that you will never again know failure, only
success.

Ryuho Okawa
President
Happy Science

PART ONE

The Source of Invincibility

1: The Source of Invincibility

1. The Qualities Required of a Leader

People are constantly trying to find out how the times they live in will evolve. They think about what is of true value, and the direction in which they should be headed, and they seek someone who can give them answers and guidance. So to be an outstanding leader, you need to be able to point others in the right direction.

Many people in this world are uncertain of how to make the best use of their abilities, their time and their money. A leader must be able to explain future trends and what people need to do in the present concisely and accurately—this is the mission of those who have truly awakened. To be a leader, what do you need to do? This will be the theme of this book.

What qualities are necessary for a leader? Firstly, you must always be able to see into the future. You need to be able to see one or two steps further than others. People regard someone who is more able to predict the outcome of events as outstanding or possessing exceptional abilities. In the same way that a very tall person is able to see much further than anyone else, people believe that someone who is outstanding is capable of seeing things more clearly because of a greatness of character, or because of spiritual abilities. Gradually, those around a person possessing these qualities will be attracted to what they see as the person's enigmatic personality, and will follow willingly.

I said that the ability to see into the future is one prerequisite for leadership, but this alone is not enough. If you foretell only the possibility of failure or give examples only of lack of success, although you may initially be regarded as a leader, people will soon drift away.

Many people have gathered at Happy Science, of which I am president, and I suppose the reason for this is that they have the expectation that if they join, something good will happen. No one would congregate in a vessel they felt was going to sink. It is because people anticipate that something good will come out of it that they join our movement and wish to be a part of it. So the second prerequisite to be a leader is an ability to make people feel that if they follow and stay close, they can expect a bright future—something good will happen.

The third prerequisite for leadership is not only to have the power to open up a bright future, but also to have enough past achievements to convince others of your standing. However, these accomplishments do not necessarily have to be a constant series of distinguished awards for excellence. No matter what kind of life you have led, people look to the way you have overcome difficulties you have faced, finding the qualities of outstanding leadership there.

If you look at the lives of great historical figures, you will notice that very few came from privileged backgrounds. Even if they had the blessing of being born into good circumstances, at some point in their lives, the tides of fortune always turned and they suffered a severe setback or faced adversity. Usually, these people were not born into a comfortable environment but developed great strength by overcoming the obstacles in their lives through their own efforts. Others find indescribable strength in the resilience of such people.

So far I have pointed out three qualities that are required of a leader. In this book, I am going to introduce "invincible thinking," a philosophy indispensable for leaders in this new era. Invincible thinking is an attitude: No matter what happens in your life, you can always find something positive, and turn any situation to your advantage. If you practice this philosophy, you will become convinced that there is no such thing as a crisis or hardship, only a continuous series of opportunities.

2. Self-Reflection Creates Leaders

Perhaps you dream of how good it would be if all your wishes could be realized, and paths opened up for you with ease. However, in actual fact, you learn more from the process of going through the ups and downs of life. Take health as an example. Some people are always full of strength and vitality; perhaps they rarely take the time to think much about their physical condition. However, if you ask whether illness, as the opposite of good health, brings only unhappiness, you will find the answer is not as negative as you may imagine.

Why is it that people occasionally fall ill? There is always an earlier stage, a preliminary period before they become sick, when they perceive the signs that something is wrong. Their bodies begin to ache, they do not feel so good, or they are not able to work as they usually do. In a sense, this is nature's way of telling to stop and rest. When people take good health for granted, they do not know how to rest unless they become ill.

When you are about to "burn out" from working too hard, it sometimes happens that you are given a temporary rest by falling ill, so you will be able to live out the full span of your days and carry out your mission. As the result of an illness, your life is in fact lengthened. If you had not become ill, you would have "burned out" and left this world before your time. So, to avoid this, your health breaks down and you are forced to undergo a period of recuperation.

What exactly is the significance of this recuperation? It is not just a period of physical rest. It is a time when you become introspective and look calmly at the inner self. When you become absorbed with outward events and concerned only about outcomes, you tend to forget to look within.

To make this easier to understand, let us take the example of a man working in the sales department of a company. When business is going well and he is bringing in lots of new accounts and customers, does he have time to think carefully about himself? Is there enough space in his mind to consider his family or other people? In most cases, the answer will be no. All he can think about is getting through each situation as it arises.

If he has set himself a target of selling fifteen automobiles a month, he will be delighted if he achieves it. He will be quite satisfied with his performance, and will, perhaps, set a target of eighteen vehicles for the following month. However, people like this who focus solely on results and whose minds are always looking outwards will eventually encounter setbacks. The reason for this is that in most cases, they forget to consider the customers, and whether they are truly happy with their purchases.

When things are going well, people tend to be preoccupied with their own satisfaction and pleasure to the exclusion of all else; in other words, they forget to consider other people's feelings. A good sale in the truest sense is a sale that continues to bring joy even after the transaction has been completed. On the other hand, if a salesperson is interested only in figures and results instead of the product itself, he or she will not realize if customers regret their purchases and feel unsatisfied.

As these sorts of people struggle to get ahead in a very competitive society, they cannot afford to care too much about others; they adopt a falsely positive attitude and judge everything by results. Not a few people believe themselves to be headed for success, unaware that they are living as a false self. These people will not achieve great stature unless they experience setbacks at some point in life. A setback may occur either at work or it may come in the form of an illness.

Nature will always provide you with opportunities for self-reflection. When this happens, you usually become intensely introspective, and this time is actually very important for your soul. Those who have never looked into the depths of the inner self or studied themselves deeply can never become true leaders.

3. Trials Are Necessary for Spiritual Growth

Returning to the example of the salesman, let us imagine that his sales record continues to increase without his showing any consideration for others until he is the top salesman in the company, and is rewarded with a promotion to the position of sales manager. Up to now he has been able to work at his own pace and has been evaluated only on results. However, now that he is the manager of the sales department, what will become of those who work under him?

He will try to make his staff adopt his methods; in other words, the only instructions he will give them are sales targets, and how many cars they should try and sell each month. If they are incapable of achieving his goals, he will consider them incapable of doing the job and see them as a burden on the company. But if they succeed, he will value them as good workers. This is the only criterion by which he is able to evaluate his staff.

On seeing their sales records, he will gradually get more and more frustrated, because although he is confident he can sell fifteen units a month, his staff are only capable of selling three to five units per month. While a good manager would take subordinates aside and teach them how to go about winning more orders, this type of manager will want to make the sales himself. He will go over the heads of subordinates, contacting customers or managers of other companies directly to make deals. The subordinates in question will become increasingly disenchanted with their job and say, "If you want to do it yourself, you're welcome to it." As a result, subordinates will not develop into efficient sales people.

The reason this particular manager behaves in this way is that he has only ever been interested in his own success. That is all he has learned; he has never really given much thought to human psychology. He has probably done his job in a selfish, pushy way. In fact, people who do well in sales departments often tend to be egotistical, and barely capable of self-analysis.

These kinds of people are quite happy to barge in on others and do business, believing they are well-liked and that everyone is open with them. However, in reality, as soon as this sort of person leaves an office, everyone heaves a sigh of relief. The person in question would never even notice. People like this have no idea how selfish they are, and they make a sales pitch with the firm belief that everyone is their friend. This is a very common story.

Subordinates who are cautious or sensitive will never be able to act as brazenly as their manager. They will not be able to follow his example or his instructions on how to do their job, so they will use their own ingenuity and draw upon their strengths. For instance, they may take up a hobby and use it as a topic of conversation to get closer to clients, or emphasize friendliness as a way of promoting sales. However, the sales manager will find this sort of approach very frustrating to watch.

People like this sales manager need to let their souls rest at some point in time; they need time to recuperate. Only when they themselves have experienced misfortune or adversity will they be able to understand the feelings of others. They usually believe themselves to be indispensable to the company and think that nothing will get done unless they are there. However, when they are ill and discover that in their absence things actually run smoothly without them, they are shocked. The biggest shock comes when their colleagues come to visit them in hospital and say, "Everything is fine in the office, so please don't worry about work." These words of comfort are actually very painful to such people, because they are really hoping that their colleagues will come and beg them to return as soon as possible so that everything will run smoothly again.

This sort of experience shatters their reality. It is as if these people were clowns; while they were completely absorbed performing their own dance beneath the spotlights, the entire audience has disappeared without their realizing. These sorts of people need to go through some kind of ordeal and it is not a backward step but an experience that is essential for them if they are to develop greater stature.

4. Learn All You Can from an Ordeal

When those who are efficient begin a new job, they go to great lengths to try and prove how well they can do it. This behavior is contrary to the "love that gives" that our Institute teaches. It is instead "love that takes," a love that craves praise. People who behave like this are eager to win the admiration of others and if they do not receive it, they try even harder. Strangely enough, the harder they try, the more they are given the cold shoulder by those around them. This is quite hard for them to understand. You, too, may have experienced that the harder you try, the less you are appreciated.

These overly eager people will eventually realize that they were actually taking love. When you see people trying hard to win praise and recognition, you feel that by giving praise, something will be drained or taken from you. When you praise someone who is trying so hard to make this happen, you feel that you are losing something.

Among those around you, you can probably easily identify the people who act as if they want praise. Are there some among your relatives or colleagues who you feel covertly desire recognition and praise? These are usually the very people you find it hardest to compliment, and so they try even harder. This vicious circle continues until eventually others begin referring to them as show-offs and this is when the dilemma starts. These people feel disappointed because although they are doing their best, no one recognizes their efforts. Then they begin to feel that the world is a very unfair place, full of people who are unable to appreciate the efforts of others.

In actual fact, when you are struggling to be recognized, you cannot see others' good points. When you are concerned only with getting the recognition for your own efforts, you tend to be under illusion that other people are just there to support you. In other words, those who are concerned only with their own success never bring happiness to others. People are very sensitive. If they do not feel happy when they are with this sort of a person, they will start to keep their distance. Then they will begin to criticize, become nasty and say negative things about a person who demands praise. This is how a situation like this steadily worsens, quite the opposite of what was hoped for.

So, even if you suffer a setback at work or the tide turns against you, do not see this negatively. It offers you the chance to strengthen your soul, while at the same time allowing you to gain a deeper understanding of other people. You may have been so self-centered that you believed the company could not function without you, but in reality you will see things running smoothly even in your absence. Unfortunately, this is the way the world works.

In business, if one person steps aside, there is always someone else to take his place. Even a president, who is often considered indispensable, soon finds someone will appear to take his or her place. In other words, in an office, a job is done not just by one person but is the result of the teamwork of staff. You can demonstrate your abilities because of the efforts of others. This is something that you must never forget.

So if you are in the throes of some setback or adversity, look back at the way you have lived for the last few years or the past few decades. Check and see that you have not allowed your life to get out of balance, or that you have not thought only of your own recognition and forgotten to give others credit for what they have done. I would like you to ponder on this.

It is very important to be able to look at yourself in this way. There are numerous occasions in life when you are presented with an opportunity to grow, and those who emit true light have undoubtedly managed to overcome hardships in the past. People who have triumphed over hardship and have been able to turn it into strength will shine from within, while those who have allowed themselves to be swept away by adversity will be forever in its shadow and give out darkness. No matter what the difficulty you face, it will not last for very long, so it is important to take advantage of the opportunity it presents, and learn all the lessons it offers.

5. Do Not Live a Life of Excuses

When faced with misfortune, make sure you do not allow yourself to feel you are the only person ever to find yourself in such circumstances. The same is true for those who are ill, and those who face a setback or failure connected to their ambitions. People tend to feel that they are the only ones who have ever had to face such a situation.

When adversity strikes, open your eyes and heart, and look at the people around you. You will realize that those who are successful are not only the people who have always known good fortune. Among them are certainly people who have experienced failure or adversity, who made the utmost effort and used their misfortune as the springboard for success.

Try to think about how many other people there must be who are in the same boat as you. There are many kinds of illnesses, for instance heart disease, cancer and numerous physical ailments. Whatever your condition, you are not the only one suffering this illness; in most cases, there will be others who are afflicted with the same condition.

Franklin D. Roosevelt (1882–1945) was the well-known President of the United States who was confined to a wheelchair. Usually people who have to depend on a wheelchair to move around find it difficult to be socially active, but despite his disability he was able to carry out his presidential duties. He was a great man in that he did not live a life of excuses, but rather did whatever he felt had to be done. He was willing to make every effort to overcome his disability.

There is another example in the United States of a woman who succeeded in reaching one of the highest positions in the country. She lost her husband when she was still young, was rejected by her children, fell into poverty and became seriously ill. Notwithstanding her miserable circumstances, she was able to rise to one of the highest positions in government.

People such as these have come to understand important lessons in life through adversity. Those who even from the depths of adversity are able to reach heights that ordinary people would never aspire to all have something in common. I would like to explain what I discovered through studying them. Firstly, they never attribute their hardships to others. They never put the blame onto other people or bemoan their fate, because they understand clearly that this would do no good whatsoever. The first key is not to blame fate or other people for any personal hardship.

Secondly, they accept what fate has given them. They do not complain, "if only that had never happened."

Instead, they accept whatever bad luck or adversity has come their way. In accepting it, they are seeing it as a reality and considering how they should go about overcoming it. They have the courage and determination to accept misfortune as a reality of life.

Thirdly, no matter what kind of adversity they face, they always find some lesson in it. They ask themselves just what it is that a difficult lesson is trying to teach them and search until they find the answer. The lesson that they learn becomes without exception a priceless treasure that remains in their hearts for a long time.

Fourthly, they never try to rely on the support of others. No matter what their disabilities, they walk the path they have been given alone, with a free and independent spirit, never forgetting to make the effort to help themselves. They accept their fate and their present state for what it is, but they do not let the status quo continue. They attempt to break out of their difficulty, relying on their own strength. All extraordinary people go through this process.

People who allow themselves to wallow in self-pity never achieve greatness, and many give in to the temptation to wallow. However, as soon as they appeal to others for sympathy, they condemn themselves to a life of continually trying to win pity. Perhaps everything went smoothly until circumstances suddenly took a turn for the worse, or perhaps you suddenly suffered some physical disability or illness. But as soon as you have the idea of depending on others to help you through, your soul is giving in to defeat. Instead, accept bravely whatever fate throws at you, and be determined to overcome it.

6. Determination and Willpower Open Up a Path

Your determination to overcome whatever fate has thrown in your way does not mean you need to undertake something huge. You just need to open a new path, starting with something close at hand. Ask yourself what you are capable of doing and what you can achieve in your current situation. If you find you are unable to use the gifts that you have developed up to now, see if you have other abilities.

What are the qualities in you your siblings, friends or teachers admired when you were young? Perhaps you have some hidden ability that even you have forgotten you possess. It is possible to open up a path to the future by finding an ability that you have not yet developed to the fullest.

I remember watching a documentary on television about a man without any arms who used to paint with his feet. He held a paintbrush between his toes, and created paintings that were of professional quality. I was very impressed. He could use his feet to do just about anything, which demonstrates that if we lose our hands, we are capable of developing our feet to the extent that they can be a substitute. This is a real-life example of someone who made a great effort.

Many people, if they were to lose the use of their hands, would give up making any further effort to help themselves and ask others to look after them for the rest of their lives. However, the man on television was different. He did not want to become dependent on others; he was able to use what was left to him to find his own way forward with determination. He liked painting so he decided to use his feet to do this and began to practice. In the beginning he could not achieve much but gradually the more he tried, the better the results, until finally he was able to produce pictures.

A person without any arms could become a painter— he was able to use his toes to hold the brushes and squeeze out the paints—and he produced real art. If this is possible, then surely people who do not have any physical disabilities can achieve anything they put their minds to. You probably received an education as a result of the support of your parents or guardians and, if you are physically healthy, there is no reason why you should not be able to achieve whatever you set your mind to.

Today, educational institutions have so many different courses offering a variety of qualifications and skills to help people achieve their goals. People like to make excuses and say, "I can't do anything in my current circumstances," or "I don't have any talent," but if they really wanted to achieve something, it would be quite possible for them to get the qualifications they needed to proceed toward their objective. The only reason they have not achieved something is that they have not made sufficient effort or they lack the willpower to reach their goals.

Surprisingly, the efforts that people with disabilities make and the process they go through to achieve their goals seem all the more wonderful when you realize what they have succeeded in overcoming. So when you hear about people with disabilities who get ahead despite adverse circumstances, what should you do? You who are overflowing with potential and energy should work harder, and give love to many more people than you do at present. Undoubtedly this is possible. The more privileged your circumstances, the greater the opportunity you have to be of service to others. I cannot stress enough how important it is always to remember this.

7. Devise Ways of Becoming Invincible

I, myself, always keep in mind that the more privileged my circumstances, the greater my opportunities to help others. However, though I intend to work harder, I sometimes feel there are physical limits to how much I can actually achieve.

Faced with these limitations, I can apply invincible thinking. If my physical limitations prevent me from accomplishing more, I need to use wisdom. That is why I constantly try to devise new ways to achieve more. This is something that you, too, can apply. Creativity, or in other words invention and discovery, are the vital elements of invincible thinking. It is true to say that the development of our organization was based on a series of creative inventions and discoveries. Whenever we came up against a brick wall or a bottleneck, we did not push recklessly ahead. Instead, we always thought carefully about the next step.

What does it mean, to be subject to physical limitations? In the light of invincible thinking, it simply means that there are limits to the sphere of your activities, so it is important to use wisdom. When you come up against limitations at work, for example, first consider whether there is some part of your job that you do not have to do yourself. Can someone else do part of it for you? This is one approach. Another is to train others to do particular tasks for you. It is quite usual to have other people take over the parts of a job that you cannot do yourself, and in doing this facilitating the overall development of the whole.

This was the way Konosuke Matsushita (1894–1989), the prominent Japanese entrepreneur who founded Panasonic, worked. He did not enjoy good health and because he was not capable of doing everything himself, he had no alternative but to entrust some of the work to others. As a result, back in the early 1930s he implemented a divisional system, an autonomous management system, for the first time in the world. This system, where the company is divided up into a number of divisions and each corporate division has its own administration, is quite often studied in business administration today. In this way, by delegating responsibility to the manager of each division, even large corporations run smoothly.

If a corporation operates with a top-down system of management, where everything is decided by the person at the top, it means that the entire operation is limited by the abilities of that one person. Once the person at the top has reached the limits of his or her abilities, the corporation can expand no further and development will grind to a halt. However, with this divisional system, the leader of each section is like the president of a small company and the corporation is structured like a conglomerate of companies. This system allowed Matsushita to achieve results that would have been impossible alone.

Because of his physical limitations, Matsushita created this system and now it has been adopted throughout the world. This is a very good example of invincible thinking. He was incapable of doing everything on his own so he turned this into an advantage. As a result, others were offered the opportunity to do more and in this way Matsushita was able to create an efficient workforce. If the president of a corporation does everything himself, his staff will not be given the opportunity to develop. Matsushita completely trusted his employees to fulfill the responsibilities he gave them, and he let them get on with the job. He thought that everyone had ability, and if he gave people free rein, they were sure to create something wonderful. This resulted in the creation of a huge company, employing hundreds of thousands of people.

The same thing happened when he created branch offices. When Matsushita decided to create a new branch some three hundred miles from the head office, he was not able to manage it directly. He said to a young man in his twenties, "I'm sorry, I can't take the train down there to help you, so you will have to carry on without me." Then he sent the young man down to run the new office.

Through experience, Matsushita came to understand that by trusting people and leaving them to get on with things themselves, they would develop into efficient workers. Here is a precedent you can follow. You should not let your own limitations restrict the work or activities of the whole. What people consider to be limitations are simply a lack of ideas. People do not lack the ability to do the work, rather they lack ingenuity and creativity.

This is something I would like you to think about. You may currently feel that you are in top form, but things will not stay this way forever. When things do not seem to be going well, instead of carrying on in the same old way, you need to pause and ask yourself if there are other ways of getting round the situation. It is always the case that whenever you try to expand the scope of your work, you will no longer be able to do everything yourself so you will need the help of others.

8. Transcend Individual Limitation

A good idea will grow only if you can find someone to work with. Suppose your job was selling fish from a truck in the streets. If you felt content doing just this, you would probably spend your whole life selling fish.

However, if you were to analyze your business, you might discover ways of getting more people to come and buy from you. You might realize that if you went to a certain residential area between four and five o'clock in the evening, you would have quite a number of customers. Compared to selling in other parts of town, you could earn five times more there for that one hour. Once you realized the sales potential of a particular time and place, it would be only natural to make a point of going there every day between those times.

Then you might wonder if there was any other time of day when demand was higher and find a lot of people arrive home and realize they have forgotten to buy groceries. Once you had discovered a potential demand, you might go looking for a suitable location to open a shop and find a place where people wanted to buy fish at a certain time in the evening. In this way, you would be able to achieve much higher sales than if you just drove around in a random fashion, waiting for people to come out and buy from you.

After a while, you would be in a position to employ an assistant. If there were two of you, you would be able to sell more fish in the same amount of time. If you went to residential areas where people came in great numbers, you would not be able to keep up. You would have to serve customers, add up bills and give people their change. If you made them wait too long, they would stop coming to you and buy their fish from other shops or the supermarket instead. However, if you had an assistant, you could concentrate on serving customers while your assistant added up the bills and handled the money. By dividing your work in this way, you would more than double your efficiency.

As sales increased, you could employ even more people. Up to this point you may have had just one truck but then you would buy a second and a third. As time passed, you would increase the number of people in each truck, expanding your business until you had perhaps five trucks working for you.

Working on your own, you would only have been able to buy small quantities of fish each day at the fish market. But as your business grew, you would be able to buy in bulk, meaning you could get better quality fish at lower prices. On your own, you may have been buying twenty or thirty mackerel a day, but as business expanded you would buy one hundred, two hundred or even five hundred mackerel, putting you in a good position to negotiate with the supplier and bring the price down. Then because you could buy your supply of fish at a less expensive rate, you could also sell it at more cheaply, satisfying your customers.

As an organization expands, it can support more and more employees, and improve the service it provides, satisfying even more customers. The bigger it gets, the more cheaply people can buy, and the better the quality of the products. In this way, everyone is happy. Then a positive cycle begins, and things can only get better. Companies that started out from nothing and grew rapidly over a period of twenty or thirty years, or which were started by a couple of workers and grew to employ thousands, are usually examples of businesses that benefited from this positive cycle.

It all boils down to whether or not you can spot potential. People who are unable to imagine various possibilities will spend thirty or forty years selling fish on their own. Those who give a lot of thought to where and when it would be best to set up shop, what they would need to do to satisfy customers, and how to serve them better, will develop and benefit from a positive cycle. Everything will go well for these businesses.

This is why, in the same line of business, one company will do well while another will not. There is always a place where the path divides, and the outcome will depend on whether you can spot an opportunity and devise ingenious method. Eighty to ninety percent of those who are unable to develop sales are limiting their business activities because of their own limitations. There are businesses that have been in the family for generations and some of them are only concerned about maintaining the status quo. As long as this is their attitude, their business will not develop.

Basically most stores, such as coffee shops, sandwich bars and hamburger restaurants, sell products of roughly the same quality. But while some of these shops develop into nationwide chains, others remain small local stores.

There are definite reasons for these differences. The truth is that the shops that expand are those where creative thinking has been used to accomplish what is beyond the capacity of just one person.

9. Two Secrets for Achieving Success

What I wanted to say in the previous section is this: "You may feel right now that you cannot move forward in life, but could the reason be simply that you are struggling alone? There is a limit to what one person can accomplish single-handedly, so if you really want to succeed in this world, you have to have other people on your side, supporting and helping you." You need to have as many people as possible willing to help. Essentially, there are two secrets to success.

1) Find a Demand

The first secret is always to be on the lookout for things people want. You should constantly have your antenna up so as to be sensitive to what people need. Businesses start wherever a demand exists. Companies that achieve rapid growth have always been started by someone who sensed a demand, and set about meeting that.

Where there is a demand, there is always work to be done. If you are working hard but find it difficult to make a profit, it is probably because there is no demand for what you are supplying. For instance, if you are running an educational institution but not many students are coming and you find it increasingly difficult to make ends meet, it is likely that there is insufficient demand and you are not providing what people want. The same is true in other types of businesses. If you cannot make a profit, it is probably because the product you are supplying does not meet local demand.

There is a traditional Japanese cake, imagawa-yaki, that has a filling of sweet bean paste, and recently one cake shop started creating new types with custard, chocolate and a variety of other fillings. As a result, the cake shop is doing extremely well and making quite a considerable profit. In its original form, the traditional Japanese sweet bean cake appealed only to the elderly and small children, but when the proprietor started making cakes with cream and chocolate fillings, people of other age groups began to buy them too. The reason the cake shop has done so well is simply that it met the needs of many more people.

This illustrates the fact that if there is a demand for a certain product, there is work to be done. This is true whether you are working for yourself, for a company, or at home. Even at home, you can try and discover your family's needs. If there is a demand, then there is always something worthwhile that needs doing. This is what you should always be on the lookout for.

2) Think about Further Development
Next, you need to consider whether this demand can be

used as a springboard to help you achieve further development. Always think of ways to continue developing your business. If you do this, you will be surprised to discover that there are always many possibilities.

Going back to the example of the shop that invented cakes with cream and chocolate fillings, after their initial success, the cake shop did not create any more new products. The owner was content with the success and stopped thinking about new products, and the result was a limit on further development. The owners are trapped by the confines of their earlier success and are not tapping into further business potential. Now that they have become successful, they must use this as a springboard to achieve greater success. It is always possible to advance to the next stage.

10. Financial Strength Provides the Power to Overcome Difficulties

Although you may think that your worries are mostly psychological, surprisingly seventy to eighty percent of those worries could be solved by achieving economic stability. I can assure you that if you were to earn ten times your present income, eighty percent of your worries would disappear. You would be amazed at how true this is.

Suppose a family complains that they always feel tired. If they look at why this is, the answer may be quite simple. The reason may be that their daily commute takes so long. As they do not have a great deal of money, the family bought a house far from the city and as a result, they have to commute long distances every day. It is hardly surprising that they feel tired all the time. If the family had some money, they could find many different solutions. They could buy a car, or they could pay someone to drive them round. This kind of problem can be solved only with money. But because of a financial lack, they become overwhelmed with complaining.

Again, a difficult situation may arise if a child or parent is ill but this too could be solved quite simply by hiring someone to help. Another worry that many parents share is the sense that their child is not doing well at school, but in some cases it is simply that the children are not receiving a good education. If they had more money, they could put their children through top notch schools, but because they are unable to do this their children may not be reaching their academic potential. If they had more money, their sons and daughters would be able to go to better schools.

In light of this, we see that the cause of most domestic problems is financial; this has been particularly true in recent years. So instead of simply worrying, you need to make an effort to find alternatives and solutions to your predicament. If your career seems to have come to a standstill and you can only expect your salary to rise with an increase in the GNP, you then need either to learn to be satisfied with what you have, or try and find some way of improving your circumstances.

Suppose you are married and your wages do not seem likely to rise; perhaps you or your partner can find some way of earning a secondary income. Maybe one of you has some hidden talent that could be put to use to improve the situation. There are people who have written books in their spare time, and to their surprise have found that what they have written sells and brings much money. There are others who discover they had some talent they did not know they possessed or who have developed skills, which as a result has brought about a sudden increase in salary. There is no telling what will lead to prosperity.

It is always important to ask yourself if there is any way you can open up a new path before you. Try not to see your present difficulties as insurmountable; rather, always be on the lookout for a chance to get ahead, and for ingenious methods of overcoming difficulties. You should not let yourself be swept away by the tides of adversity, nor should you just complain about your situation. Instead try to accept adversity and use it as a springboard to find ways of moving forward and making further progress.

11. Discover the Invincible Self

Is it possible that you are putting limits on your own abilities? Are you allowing yourself to be controlled by the past? Are you holding on to fixed ideas or assumptions about yourself? If this is the case, unfortunately you will end up living your entire life according to those fixed ideas.

People who put limits on themselves will never become more than they think they are. It is important always to believe that you have the potential to do better than you are now. As I have explained over and over, at every opportunity, the power of the will is very significant. "You are what you think," is an eternal truth, so it is important that you make increasing use of the power of the will from now on.

There is one facet in particular of the power of the will that I would like to consider. I have talked about financial stability, and I have said that when you are faced with a problem that stems from lack of money, you should make an effort to overcome it. However, another problem that seems to trouble a lot of people is an inferiority complex connected to educational achievements or educational background.

Perhaps this is troubling you right now. The fact that you were unable to go on to a particular high school or university decades ago may be preying on your mind; perhaps you have lived your whole life in its shadow. There are many people still worrying about their educational background twenty or thirty years on. However, if you still have an inferiority complex after twenty or thirty years, it is only natural for others to consider your educational background unsatisfactory because you yourself continue to regard it as such.

There are many people in this world who have managed to make a success of their lives despite the fact they did not receive any formal education after graduating from junior high school. I am sure they did not say to themselves, "I did not manage to go to senior high school because I am not smart enough, so I can only do menial jobs." In one major Japanese global trading company, there was a man who did not go to senior high school and nevertheless finally became vice-president of the company, responsible for all finances. He managed to achieve this position despite a lack of formal education, which indicates that he must have made two or three times more effort than anyone else to make up for his lack of knowledge.

There are also a lot of people who suffer an inferiority complex because they were unable to keep up with their university studies. It is quite common for people today to have a complex about their lack of intellectual ability. However, if something that happened years ago is your only excuse for failing now, then you cannot complain that you have been treated unfairly. It is what you have been able to do and what you have achieved since then which is important.

Most people study for an average of four years at university, and no matter how hard they work while they are there, the amount they can learn in such a short time is quite limited. Even if you find learning difficult, if you study for ten years, you will be able to master what someone else learned in four. If you cannot grasp it completely in ten years, then surely you can manage it in twenty. No matter how difficult you find learning, if you continue to make an effort for twenty years, you will certainly be able to master any subject.

So what is important is how you have lived since you completed your education, and whether you have achieved the sort of results that will imbue you with confidence. In the majority of cases, people tend to use a lack of education as an excuse. However, I must point out that their weakness is not their inadequate education, but the fact that their thinking remains stuck in the past.

If you are really upset and feel your education was inadequate, it is very important to make an effort to compensate for it, and to put in the time to do this. In most cases, if you spend three times as long as others, you should be able to achieve your goal. If someone else can accomplish something in two or three years, then there is absolutely no reason why you should not be able to accomplish it in ten. What prevents you from accomplishing this is your lack of effort and conviction.

Everyone suffers from some sort of inferiority complex. If you live your life consumed by your own inadequacies, then inevitably others will consider you merely someone who suffers from some sort of inferiority complex. Only when you make sufficient effort to overcome feelings of inferiority can you finally cast them off. I hope you will not use these sorts of feelings as an excuse.

People who lack formal education share one characteristic; they have difficulty making generalizations and grasping an overall picture. You may wonder why this is. The reason is that after they leave school, they work in one specialized job, or they experience only one field of work. In many cases, they have only thought about their specialty. Because they have not had the opportunity to be exposed to a basic general education, they have difficulty seeing the broader perspective. Just as the branches of a tree cannot grow without the trunk, they are unable to broaden their perspective because they have not received a basic education. This is their weakness.

If you are worried that your weakness lies in intelligence, firstly do not complain that your abilities are limited. Instead, try to make an effort to learn, to adopt a wider perspective, and to achieve some understanding of a wide range of topics. Once you have managed to do this, you will find there is no longer any need to suffer this inferiority complex.

At Happy Science, we have opportunities to learn the Truth through Level Seminars that consists of three different levels of tests, and the results of these tests do not always reflect a person's academic background. There are a lot of people who have studied hard at school but who, as time goes on, become less discerning. On the other hand, there are many who at first do not seem so bright, but later prove to be quite sharp. These people are not aware of how they have changed in the ten or twenty years since they graduated. But the results people produce reveal how they have trained themselves intellectually since graduating from school.

I sincerely hope that you are not limiting yourself, and I truly believe that you become what you think you are. Integrate this into your life today and manifest your thoughts by making the necessary effort. Progress steadily, one step at a time, as if you were climbing steps or the rungs of a ladder one at a time. As you continue doing this, I guarantee that a path will open up before you, and you will discover the self that is always victorious and invincible.

PART TWO

❧ *Revolutionizing Your Perspective* ❧

2. Revolutionizing Your Perspective

1. The Importance of Creating New Ideas
In this chapter, I would like to talk about the importance of the way in which we think. You may have read other religious books in the past and noticed that the majority of them tend to focus on the duality of good and evil, the good heart and the evil heart, good thoughts and evil thoughts, good actions and evil actions, and so forth. Religions all share this propensity for duality, and when they speak of human beings they divide them into good and bad, with the teaching that when they die they will go either to heaven or hell.

People, particularly those interested in spiritual matters, quickly perceive the difference between good and evil and so they tend to think in a dualistic way. As a result, they have a tendency to divide everything into black and white. Some do not feel secure unless they categorize what is around them, including people and circumstances, as good or evil. Regrettably, when you look at the world in this way, there is the possibility of dismissing things that hold great potential. This is quite a loss.

Let us imagine, for example, that beings from outer space came to Earth in their flying saucer and landed in a country in the middle of a rainy season. Perhaps they would step out of their spaceship and think to themselves, "Well, we have come all this way yet it does nothing but rain on this planet. There is nothing here for us so let's leave as quickly as possible." Dissatisfied with the planet, they depart without a second thought. They have left no room for possibilities, for discovering Earth's potential or what they could do on it.

However, despite the fact that it does at times rain on Earth, there are also days which are beautiful and sunny. The question is whether the beings from outer space are aware of this. If they were to experience a glorious spring day, they would think this planet was not so bad and that it might be a good place to live. But if they arrived on a day when it was pouring with rain and straightaway assumed that the planet was not a good place to be, then all further possibilities would end right there.

With their preconceived ideas, they would deny all further potential and fly away in their spacecraft, once again traveling through space, looking for somewhere else to land. This would take a lot more effort. Had they remained on Earth at least a month, the rainy season would have come to an end. But unable to wait that long, they leave to continue traveling through space for many

more years. This kind of attitude creates worry unneces-
sarily.

I am using beings from outer space as an example, but
I am sure that you do the same thing. If you are married,
for instance, have you ever thought that you would be
happier if you had married someone else? Answer this
honestly. I suppose at least fifty percent of those who are
married think, "if only my wife were someone else," or "if
only I had chosen a different husband." Although I said
more than fifty percent, perhaps the number of people who
think like this could easily be eighty or ninety percent of
all couples.

They know that they should not think this way, but
somewhere in their hearts they feel that if only they could
change partners, or if only they had realized earlier what
they were getting themselves into they could have enjoyed
a completely different life. They carry on thinking like this
for decades, but it does no good whatsoever. Although
they may not realize it, their thinking is exactly the same
as the beings from outer space who landed on Earth in the
middle of the rainy season.

What is important in this situation is to change your
outlook; in other words, adopt a new way of thinking.
Always ask yourself if there is some other way of seeing
a situation. Another important point is to be willing to
make the effort to devise new ways of improving a situation. It is very important to practice doing this.

2. Find a Third Alternative

The concept of "revolutionizing your perspective" may sound very difficult, but all it really means is to find a new way of doing things. This framework can be applied to people in all walks of life.

Let me tell you how I apply this. Over the last few years, there has been a tremendous increase in the number of times I have stood in front of a large audience to speak. At the same time, I have been writing books. Authors generally find it hard to write if they have to leave their writing space often. This is true of all writers for the simple reason that they cannot find the time to devote to writing. To get around this, they will often move to the mountains or travel somewhere so that they can hide or disappear; then they can apply themselves to their work. Unless they cut down on social obligations, they are unable to write.

This of course applies as much to me as to anyone else. I was faced with the dilemma of whether to give lectures or to settle down to writing. However, there was another way to look at the situation; that was to ask myself whether these two activities were really at odds with one another, or whether they were in fact compatible. Then I realized there was a way to achieve both.

You will understand how I managed this when I tell you that I often compile a series of lectures and make a book out of them. This book, *Invincible Thinking*, is based on a series of four lectures that I gave. I deliver lectures once every two or three weeks, and speak for approximately an hour and twenty minutes each time. Afterward, these lectures can be collected to make a book. Using this technique, I am able to produce books without having to lock myself away in a room to write. This is one idea for solving this dilemma.

You may wonder if all authors produce books in this way; they do not. The reason is that spoken and written language are not the same, so it is not sufficient just to transcribe a talk and put it onto paper. Authors like to use a proper written style so they are quite specific about their choice of adjectives, conjunctions and closing sentences. As long as they are concerned about these kinds of things, they will never be able to transfer the spoken word onto paper so they will not compile their lectures to create a book.

However, there is also a way of letting go, trying to do the best you can with spoken language, and giving up your attachment to the written style. There is absolutely no reason why a book has to be written in a perfect literary style in the first place, as long as readers are able to learn something from what they read. As long as the contents are transmitted to the reader in an easy-to-read fashion, surely this is sufficient. With practice, it is quite possible to create a good book in this way, and the only reason people think it is not possible is that they adhere to an excessively literary style. If they are willing to let go of this, there is no reason why public speaking and writing cannot be compatible.

Of course, there has to be a certain amount of ingenuity. If a single lecture is to become the chapter of a
book, for instance, I have to have enough content to be
able to talk for one and a half hours. Let me explain how
I go about ensuring this. As a result of my past training, I
am able to read through a book marking a couple of lines
from each page with a red pen and memorizing all the
passages I have marked. While I do not remember the bulk
of the text, the essence of a book stays in my mind to be
recalled at will. This is the way my memory works.

Having trained myself to do this, I am also able to add
red lines mentally while I talk. By this I mean that I can
tell which parts of my speech people will want to mark in
red after it has been transcribed into book form. If there
are approximately two lines like this on every page, it will
become a book worth reading. Quite simply, if there are
two lines worth remembering on each page, it will make a
good book and readers will not feel that they have wasted
their time. This skill can be developed with training.

This is how I have revolutionized my perspective in
my own career. Although you are not in the same position
as I am and you do not have the same opportunities, this is
a philosophy that you also can use in your life. If you look
into your heart, do you find two impulses that contradict
each other?

Suppose there are two options, A and B. If you decide
to do A, option B has to be put aside. Yet if you choose B,
option A will have to be given up. Everyone faces these

kinds of dilemmas and they can cause a lot of anxiety. For instance, let us say that you wish to go to a seminar at our organization but if you go, your partner will be a little upset at being left behind, and this may cause disharmony at home. If you decide not to go, your relationship with your partner will be harmonious but you will feel frustrated because you really want to go. You find yourself in many situations like this; in this case, you could simply take your partner with you to the seminar, or look for other options to solve the dilemma.

When you find yourself suffering as a result of two opposing desires or needs like this, do not allow yourself to be driven to the point where you have to decide between one or the other. Tell yourself that there has to be a way of bringing the two contradictory elements together or even finding a third option which will allow you to avoid the problem altogether. You just have to continue thinking of new ways to get around the problem. If you keep trying to find new ways of overcoming the difficulty, a path is sure to open up before you.

The more you practice, the more new ways you will come up with to free yourself from a dilemma. This kind of mental exercise is important and if you make a habit of thinking like this, you will find that the chances of coming up with a good idea increase dramatically. You will achieve a certain level of skill at doing this.

Once you have this ability, you will find that whenever you are faced with a problem, you will be able to say to yourself, "Well, the problem lies in this and this. There are two contradictory possibilities, but if I manage this problem in such and such a way, things should turn out OK. If that does not work, then I can try another option." In this way, you will be able to come up with a solution in a matter of seconds, and you will have no more problems; only the expectation of potential solutions will remain. If your first solution does not pan out, then you can fall back on the second possible solution, then the third. With these in hand, you will be left with absolutely nothing to worry about.

If you do this mental exercise, you will no longer see problems simply as a question of choosing between a good and a bad outcome; you will realize that every problem you face, both in your environment and in your relationships with those around you, can be solved by finding a different approach. It is a very interesting experience.

3. Think in the Opposite Way to Create Positiveness

While we are on the subject of mental exercises, I would like to consider efficiency at work. Although you probably work very hard at your job, you may sometimes feel as if you are never able to catch up with all your work. For the most part, people who feel this way have simply become slaves of habit, and their efficiency at work has usually become extremely low.

This kind of person does not know how to sit back and enjoy life, and usually does not ever take a summer holiday. In some parts of the world, this will strike a chord. I am sure that there are people who have to work right through their holidays, who think that if they were to take so much as a single day off, someone else would have to do their job for them, which would not be fair. With this sort of attitude, it is hardly surprising some of these people decide not to take holidays. They tell others to go ahead and take a holiday, but they feel it is impossible for they themselves to do so. This gradually festers in their minds until it becomes a form of self-punishment. These people even end up offering to do other people's work for them and then suffer; as a result they become even less efficient in their own jobs.

Consider what would happen in this situation if you were just to go ahead and take a holiday. Even in companies where a three-day holiday is considered the absolute maximum and taking any more would lead to a serious dispute, still think about taking a whole week off. If you do end up taking a week's vacation, the first thing that springs to mind will be how the work you do every day will pile up on your desk, making life difficult for both your colleagues and clients.

The next thing you will think about is what others will think of you. This is probably the main reason you do not want to take any time off. You do not want to be thought of as lazy or as someone who only ever thinks of themselves. There again, you may imagine others will secretly complain that they have to do your work on top of their own so you will decide that you cannot take any time off. I imagine this is the main reason these sorts of people do not take holidays. In the end, they give in to the majority and settle for just a two-day holiday.

However, there is another way of thinking. If you are in this situation, ask yourself if there might be some way you can take a holiday without putting your colleagues to extra trouble, and still benefit yourself. You may find it is in fact possible. For instance, if you want to take a holiday in August, aim to finish all the work that you are responsible for before that. If you make the effort, you will find this is quite possible. Push yourself until you are in a position where you have no work left to do. Carry on until you can look around and say, "Work? I haven't got any. I am finished up until the end of the year."

To achieve this, you will have to work extremely efficiently for the next month. Although it would be enough to finish all your work by August, you must try to clear your desk before this. Even if you do all your work ahead of time, there is still the chance that on your return from holiday you will come in for criticism from jealous colleagues, so you should make the effort to finish all of September's work as well. This means you have to do an awful lot of work in advance.

Once you have managed this, you will realize that although you thought you were busy every day and had enough work to last you for several months, you were in fact mistaken. The truth is that unconsciously, you were scared you would run out of things to do if you worked too hard, so you always put a certain amount of work aside just in case. You were worried that there might not be enough to keep you busy each day so you averaged it out to make it last. However, if you put your mind to it, it is quite possible to finish it all ahead of time.

Some people have a guilty conscience if they go on vacation, but they should use these feelings of guilt as an incentive to work even harder. If you worry that you might be ostracized by your colleagues when you return, you should simply work all the harder. Then not only will you be able to finish all your work up to the end of the year, but you will also be able to clear your desk until March of the following year. Once you have accomplished all this, you need have no fear of what anyone else might say about you. So depending on your attitude, what you had considered an obstacle can be used as a springboard to spur you on to greater things.

Another problem with taking a holiday is that you may feel your colleagues will have trouble doing their work if you are not there, but you should use this as an opportunity to make it quite clear exactly what your job involves. You are probably usually able to cope with your work in your own way without giving others much thought, but if you are not going to be there, you will need to be able to give others a clear idea of what you do. If someone else has to take your calls and do your work, they need to be able to proceed as if you were there.

To achieve this, you need to create a manual that explains everything in a clear and concise way. Be able to say, "Please manage this situation in this way," so that other people can tell at a glance what they need to do to cover for you. So before you leave for your vacation, list everything and say, "At the moment, we have these problems, please go about solving them in this way. If you receive a phone call from so-and-so, say the following." In this way, everything is clear and you can leave for your holiday.

However, if you were not to bother with any of this, and just went off on holiday without any preparations, saying to your colleagues, "Oh! I'm off from tomorrow! See you!" then it is only to be expected that your colleagues would be angry. If they received a phone call from one of your clients demanding an answer to something you had not informed them about beforehand, you could hardly blame them for bearing grudges later. People would no longer trust you, and you would have only yourself to blame.

You can see that something which may appear detrimental to your work or irreconcilable with your position can, in fact, serve to improve your efficiency or even raise the standard of your work. No matter what field you work in, this always applies. If you work in a store, dealing with customer after customer all day, you may think you are too busy and even complain to others about how busy you are. But if you give the matter some thought, you will realize that the really busy periods come in cycles. You may think you are rushed off your feet twelve hours a day, but if you consider this honestly, you will realize that in fact you also enjoy periods when you do not have much to do. When you realize there are lulls in your work, you should use your ingenuity and make use of them to do something else.

People who work in a cafeteria or a restaurant, for example, may think that they are busy all day but in actual fact, although they are busy from about noon to two o'clock, the next busy period does not begin until around five in the evening. In between there is a lull. If they were to rationalize their workload, it might be possible for them to take a break for a couple of hours in the afternoon. Of course, if you suggest this to them, they will tell you that they are busy all afternoon preparing for the evening rush. Perhaps they could prepare for evening in the morning. Again, they will tell you that they are busy in the mornings preparing for lunchtime, but in actual fact most of them have never given the matter any thought. They have just accepted that the way they do things is the only way, but if they were to do more at one time, it would leave them free time later in the day.

There are many such examples, and I would like you all to think of ways of getting around difficult situations. In doing so, I would like you to free yourself from your worries, one at a time.

4. Use Failure as a Springboard

In the course of your life, you will often face moments when you have to make decisions about whether to go forward or backward, take the path to the right or the path to the left. At these times, people who can only respond in a yes-no fashion will find themselves sucked into whirlpools of despair and often they become discouraged. Instead of limiting your decision-making to a simple yes or no choice, I would like you always to try to find a third option. This is extremely important and the difference between the lives of those able to think in this way and those who are not will be quite marked.

The idea of a "batting average" that is used in baseball cannot be applied exactly to life, but I can safely say that people who always search for a third option will have at least a thirty percent "batting average." Or, to use the metaphor of a percentage of wins, those who win thirty to forty percent of the time, in other words people who lose more often than they win, will be able to increase their wins by another thirty to forty percent through adopting this way of thinking, even if they do not win one hundred percent of the time.

Although the final results may not be what you were hoping for, your thoughts all through that time will stand you in good stead for the next stage. You may be defeated on that occasion and say to yourself, "although I did my best to find a way out by revolutionizing my perspective, things didn't work out as I would have wished." However, the effort you have made to think of all the possible alternatives is not a complete waste; when you face a different problem in a year, in two years or even in five years time, you will be able to find alternative solutions in another situation. The benefit of this effort is that once you have clarified your thoughts, you will be able to use these ideas next time.

To explain "revolutionizing your perspective" from another angle, it means thinking in a way that turns every situation to your advantage, even failure. It is an attitude where no matter what happens, you can always turn it into an opportunity to take the next step forward. If you experience failure, think of how you can use it as a lever with which to achieve something positive. This is one aspect of putting into practice a revolution in perspective. Think how you can use all the resources within your reach. Nothing is ever wasted; you can make use of every event and situation that occurs in your life.

The same applies to people. There are some people you like and some you do not. When you are with someone you like, you will feel joyful and happy. When, on the other hand, you meet someone you dislike, they will become your personal tutor, because you can make an exhaustive study, working out why their personality is so disagreeable to you. It is important to be grateful to have the opportunity to learn more about human nature. Try and find out why they make so many mistakes, why their character so displeases you, why they say such terrible things, or why they have such a pessimistic view of everything. If you study every facet of their personality, you will learn a great deal from them.

The lessons you learn from studying others become your personal savings. Do not regard a deposit simply as the money you put into a bank. The lessons you have learned and confirmed for yourself, through your own experiences and by observing others, are stored as your own "deposit" which can later be referred to as the occasion requires. People with a rich supply of these "deposits" will be successful in life. I cannot stress the importance of this attitude enough.

5. There Is No Waste in the World Created by God

One more point I would like to make is that revolutionizing your perspective is not confined solely to individual concerns. Although the idea is closely connected to self-realization, it is not a way of thinking simply to help you achieve personal ambitions or make your life easier. This is something I would like you to know at the outset.

The basis of this thinking is the idea that there is absolutely nothing in this world that God created that is not of use. Living as human beings in this world, people moan, complain, have many different desires and think of this world as a difficult place to live. Some people even feel they cannot trust anyone they meet. However, revolutionizing your perspective is based on the belief that these kinds of negative views cannot be true. Unless you adopt this as your premise, you cannot revolutionize your perspective.

This world was created by God and He created it with the best of intentions. He intended it to be a marvelous place, good, beautiful and pure, otherwise He would not have created it at all. It is true that people often seem to be faced with problems, and they must confront what in their eyes seems evil. But this was not God's intention.

In my books, you will read that the world we inhabit did not appear by accident; it is God's creation. You will also learn that it was created by the great and holy will of God. If this is so, why should you experience discomfort or pain while you live in it? Probably because you do not believe that the world was created with the best of intentions to begin with. You may not have understood that God created it believing it to be a good and wonderful place. You may be suffering because you misunderstand this truth, or because your perceptions are distorted.

When you see the world in this light, your thinking will change. You will realize that up to now, you have put yourself in a position of judging the world and criticizing other people. Perhaps you have blamed fate and passed judgment on all sorts of things around you, categorizing them as either good or evil and concluded that there is more that harms than helps you. As a result, you may have come to believe that the world is a dark and evil place. However, go back to the starting point: This is the world

God created. To believe that this world created by God is
a wonderful place is the very beginning of everything. It is
only your wrong understanding and your distorted views
that prevent you from thinking in this way.

Once you are able to think like this, you will start to
ask whether your way of looking at life and your attitudes
could be mistaken. Perhaps you think that other people are
not good or that there are a lot of untrustworthy people in
this world, but you will start to feel that this kind of
thinking is wrong. If the basic premise is that the world
has been created on a foundation of goodness, then an attitude of blaming what is around you is mistaken.

The main problem lies in incorrect perception of the
world that you live in and what you have been given.
Everything that exists is here for you as nourishment, to
enrich your soul. Once you adopt this way of thinking, you
will understand that nothing in this world is a waste.

6. Confront Your Karma with a Positive Attitude

The basic premise that the world you live in was created by
God leads to the next premise, which you may have
already heard about, the law of reincarnation. If you accept
the idea that all human beings incarnate in this world
repeatedly to further their spiritual growth, then you are
able to interpret your current situation, which you may see
as an ordeal, differently. If you base your thinking on the
fact that you have eternal life, and are born again and again
on earth, then you will have a completely new perspective.

You will realize that the problems you face right now reveal what kind of challenges you have to overcome in this life. Life is like a workbook of problems to be solved and what is causing you suffering right now, especially the deepest suffering, is showing you the life issues that you have been given. So even if you feel that you are being swept away in a whirlpool of suffering, it actually means that right now you are facing one of the most important issues in your life, and you are currently experiencing a crucial time for your spiritual growth. This is an exciting time for you.

You have at last entered the ring for the match. Up to now you may have spent a long time in training, shadow-boxing with an imaginary opponent, but that time is now over and the match is about to begin. When the referee shouts for the fighter in the red corner, it is time for you to take off your gown and enter the ring. Once you are in the ring, you may think to yourself something like, "I've got to go to the bathroom," but it is too late for that. Once you have been called, you must take your place in the ring and fight.

If you are in the thick of some difficulty right now, it means that after practicing for this title match for a month, two months, maybe even six months, you have finally entered the ring. This is the moment you were born into this world for; in fact, even before you were born you may have spent decades or even centuries in the other world preparing for this moment. Only when you felt strong

enough did you decide to come down to Earth and meet
this challenge. You may have spent centuries, or in some
cases, much longer building up to this time. You have
devoted so much time to training for the big match.

So after you have entered the ring, it is too late to start
making excuses. Once you are in there, you know what
you have to do. You have an opponent in front of you so
do not worry about anything else; you have no choice but
to knock the opponent out. If your opponent were a
person, he might hit back and this could be very painful.
But what you are faced with is not a human being. What
you see as an insurmountable problem is in fact nothing
more than a mirage. It is simply your own karma
appearing before you in the form of some problem or
worry. What you are fighting in the ring is not another
person; it is a battle between you and your karma, and you
have to win this match at all costs. This is the purpose of
your present incarnation.

This is simply explaining "revolutionizing your
perspective" from a different angle. It is a way of
explaining this idea from the standpoint of courage and
enthusiasm. For instance, if you think of yourself as
climbing into the ring, you cannot help but feel encour-
aged. After all, this is the fight you have trained for all
these years. So why is it that now, when the crucial
moment has come, you are still making excuses, saying
things like "I can't help it if I'm not very intelligent," or
"It's all because of my circumstances," "Blame it on my

parents," "It was my brother's fault," or "I cannot succeed because I am poor."

You are in the ring, you have come out of the red corner, touched gloves with your opponent in the blue corner and now you are glaring at each other. Making excuses is the equivalent of someone in that position saying, "Well, actually, I haven't done any training recently. My legs are a little stiff and my back has been sore since yesterday. My shoulder is all swollen and I can hardly walk. And I've got no muscles, see? I don't have any fighting spirit either. It's all my trainer's fault that I haven't done any training. Well you know, when I think about it, it makes no difference to me whether I win or lose this match anyway. Anyhow, everyone thinks that I am going to lose..." If you heard this from an opponent, you would think that this person was weak and give him a good punch in the face!

This kind of attitude is no good. Once you are in the ring, you have to hide your weaknesses and give it your best shot. The moment you find yourself face to face with your karma, you have to be determined to put on a brave face and go for it. Even if you are at a disadvantage, do not show it. Do not let your opponent know he has a chance. Though you may only weigh a hundred and forty pounds, you must stick out your chest and behave as if you weighed more, to make your opponent afraid you will knock him out. You always need to think positively.

7. People Assess You Differently

Many people have an inferiority complex about their
body. Very few think that they have a perfect body. In
actual fact, not many people have a flawless physique, so
there is little point worrying about your physical short-
comings.

If you were to list all the things that worry you, how
many worries do you think you could come up with? I am
sure your concerns would be about both your physique
and your character, but in most cases you probably could
not come up with more than twenty, or thirty at most. You
would have to be a genius to come up with one or two
hundred. If you can really think of one hundred worries
that have to do with your physique, and a hundred more
worries to do with mental and spiritual shortcomings, that
is very impressive. However, you need to ascertain
whether, in actual fact, you really do worry about them all.

Many of the things you may believe are negative
factors in your life are actually quite the opposite, and this
is something I would like you to consider very carefully.
Are you sure that the things you are worrying about do not
have some positive aspect? If you are able to see the positive side, make an effort and develop it.

8. Plan to Live to One Hundred and Twenty

A number of people worry that they are not clever enough,
not sufficiently intelligent. Having become aware that
they lack knowledge, if they simply conclude that they are

no good, there will be no chance of them changing them-selves. Sometimes it is important to teach people where their limits lie, but then they should say to themselves "that is why it is worth making an effort." If you feel a lack of intellectual ability, you can study continuously and this can become an enjoyable endeavor. No matter how long you study for, you will never run out of new material. This is one way of approaching the problem.

I have already written well over one hundred books—some people are able to read fast and grasp the contents quickly. From a different perspective, I feel sorry for them, because their enjoyment is over in such a short time. On the other hand, there are people who plan to read all the books over a ten-year period. Those who have a long-term plan like this are blessed. Each year more books are published than they are able to read, so their schedule is always being pushed back and extended; they will have no choice but to live for a very long time to complete the mountain of books before them. This means that they are much more fortunate than those who die early.

I would especially like those in their fifties or sixties, whose careers are gradually winding down, to think once more about their life span. Are you sure that you do not imagine you have only another five or ten years of life left? That would be tragic. People tend to be pessimistic about the length of their lives, and say that if they have only ten more years then there is no point in thinking about starting anything new.

However, I would like you to increase your life expectancy. You should make plans to live to the age of about a hundred and twenty. This is particularly true for middle-aged people; they should look forward to living until they reach a hundred and twenty. If they do this, what they need to do will become quite clear. For instance, if they are now sixty, they will have another sixty years to live, and so they have to plan what they intend to do during this period.

Are they content to live without some new purpose in life? If they have another sixty years to live, it is the same as starting out on a new life as a baby. In another ten years, they will be teenagers, then young adults. At about ninety, they will enter a phase when they will experience romance in their lives, then at one hundred... All kinds of things have yet to happen for them, so they need to start thinking about them now. If they should have the misfortune to pass away in their spiritual youth, when they are only ninety, what is there to regret? Nothing at all.

So those who think they do not have long to live need to revolutionize their perspective, and make plans to live to a hundred and twenty. If people in their sixties do this, it means they have another sixty years to go. If there is no change to the plan, my life on Earth will last another fifty years, so they have ten years more than I do to continue studying. They will be fortunate enough to able to complete their study of all my lectures and books on the Truth before they leave this world.

Consider your present age, then make plans for a much longer life. This is how I would like you to plan for your future.

9. Life Can Be Extended through Effort

It is a fact that you can extend your life through effort. It is said that the span of a persons life is already fixed, but this is not one hundred percent true. In the course of your life, you come to several turning points which mark the start of new phases; these are, to a certain degree, prearranged. There are many turning points, for example, at fifty-five, seventy, seventy-five, eighty years old and so on. However, it is rather like the probability factor in weather forecasting; it is eighty percent or perhaps fifty or sixty percent certain, but not fixed. If you are able to achieve some sort of revolution in your thinking at these turning points, you may be able to extend your own life.

If you can offer some reason why you should remain in this world, you can extend your life here. If you are unable to do this, you have to leave. But if you can demonstrate some reason for your continued presence, you will be allowed to remain on Earth. So if you who wish to live longer, you need to have some reason for your continued presence. The most common reason is that you still have work to do, so you should make plans for your future.

I feel the need to give teachings for those in the prime of life, but if I were to say what is most essential, it is deciding that your desired life span is one hundred and twenty years. If you decide you are going to live to this age, you will find that most of your worries disappear. You will know exactly what you have to do, and you can set about accomplishing it little by little. It is important to go ahead, regardless of whether or not your life will end while you are in the middle of it.

If you are still in your twenties, you have a lot of work to do. If you have a hundred years of life left, you will have to make a lot of plans to fill all the time that is ahead of you. One hundred years is too long to accomplish just one plan, so young people need to have plans for several paths they would like to take in their lifetime. They have to make many different kinds of preparations to be able to enjoy a hundred years more life.

Life is like a fireworks display; if there were only one kind of fireworks, it would be boring. You need to prepare two, three, four different kinds of fireworks, and now and again a rocket would be nice. It is important to prepare a number of different sorts of plans for the future. Eventually, at thirty, forty, fifty or sixty years of age, your life may start to bloom, so you need to sow a variety of seeds.

By doing this, you will attain greater stature and strengthen the foundations of your knowledge and understanding. If you simply collect information that can be used straightaway, this will not add to your overall stature because what simply passes by in the course of a life cannot be stored as knowledge. The richness of your soul can be cultivated only by continual learning what is certain to enrich you, regardless of whether or not it will help you in the future. To acquire this richness, a grand-scale life plan is essential.

Even if all your studies, your experience, your knowledge and the learning you have accumulated are not directly useful in your lifetime, nothing is wasted. You may wonder what you can take with you when you return to the other world and I can tell you: Everything that you have learned in the course of your life. You can take it with you because it has been assimilated within. Although it may not benefit you while you are alive, from a long-term perspective, it benefits you to have learned so much in one life.

PART THREE

Life and Victory

3: Life and Victory

1. When a Philosophy Radiates Light

I have entitled Part Three "Life and Victory." One of the characteristics of this book, *Invincible Thinking*, is that it is not just abstract theory; because the theme is how to achieve continual victory in life, it needs to be a practical guide.

When you are faced with a difficult situation, you probably want to know what you need to do in practical terms. Most people are looking for an answer to the question, "What should I do? How should I go about solving this problem?" Once your problems have been solved, you will find that most of your worries have disappeared and you will reach the next stage in your development, moving forward in your life in a positive way.

For this reason, I certainly do not underestimate the importance of philosophy or Truth on the practical level. Although the theme of this book may be practical, everyday matters, if it succeeds in bringing people salvation and happiness, then so much the better. I have no

intention of being active on only a philosophical level; I
believe that only when a philosophy has the power to actually save large numbers of people does it give out light.

In this part of the book, I will consider what you need
to master and the minimum number of obstacles you must
overcome to be victorious in life. I have arranged these
under the headings: "How to Live a Healthy Life," "The
Creation of Wealth," "Spouse and Home," "Encounters
That Will Change Your Destiny," and "A Spiritual
Legacy," and I will tackle each of these in turn.

While these themes will not allow you to learn everything that you need to be victorious in life, I am sure that
they will enable you to reach a stage where you can overcome most basic problems. A lot depends on how far you
are able to put the principles from the examples I give into
practice, and whether you are able to use them as a central
pillar around which to structure your own experiences.

2. How to Live a Healthy Life
1) Physical Conditions Restrict the Mind
I would like to start by discussing the theme, "how to live
a healthy life." When thinking about victory in life, health
is a subject that cannot be avoided.

I have written well over one hundred books that have
looked at problems related to the mind from many
different angles. I have also gone beyond the individual to
discuss the mind of the Grand Cosmos. Although there are

any number of grand themes, all of them inevitably start with the individual human being.

Essentially all human beings are spiritual beings; at the same time, we cannot deny that we are living now in this three-dimensional world (this world). Although we are beings of the Real World (the other world) and that is our true state, at present we are inhabitants of this world and as such we have to take on a form suitable for life in this realm.

When I say this, I mean that we have to express ourselves through the physical body. Even high spirits have no alternative but to use a physical body to express themselves when they are here on Earth. They cannot express themselves solely through the brilliance of the light they radiate. Even if they do give out light, they still have to communicate by talking with their mouths, appealing with their eyes, using the brain to write what they think, so they too are restricted by a physical form.

This is a very important issue. My teachings do not deny the physical form; we do not say that because matter does not exist, we do not have to bother about the physical body. Our current teachings deal with the concerns of the three-dimensional world and how human beings at present on this Earth should live, so we cannot afford to ignore issues that concern the physical body.

When talking specifically about the mind, we cannot ignore spiritual influences that affect everyone without exception. How to overcome negative spiritual influences is a major issue for each individual, and it is true that self-reflection is a very effective technique for achieving this. However, there is something we have to consider even before we begin self-reflection, and that is the fact that the mind is not independent but bound by a set of conditions.

One of these conditions is the physical body. If you do not have good control over your physical state, it will bring pressure to bear on the mind causing it to move in wrong directions.

2) Learn to Control Your Physical Body

Your body is like a bicycle that you have learned to ride well. Do you remember how it felt when you first sat on a bike? You probably could not understand how you were supposed to ride such an unstable contraption.

When you were a child, I am sure that you first learned to ride with training wheels. These are the small wheels that attach to either side of the rear wheel to give the bicycle some stability while you are getting used to riding it. A bicycle with these wheels seems very stable. However, when these training wheels are removed leaving only the two big wheels front and back, the bicycle seems so unstable that it becomes extremely difficult to ride. You do not know how to keep your balance. Simply balancing is hard enough on its own, but at the same time you also have to pedal to make the bike move forward. That is not

all, you have to look left and right, and when you come to
a junction you have to decide which direction you want to
go. When you come to a slope, you have to make an effort
to get up it, and then you have to use the brakes to control
your speed as you come down the other side.

Seen in this way, it is hardly surprising that you used
to think of the bicycle as an unstable and downright
dangerous machine. However, once you become used to
riding one every day, it almost becomes an extension of
your body and you can ride it without the slightest difficulty. Physical bodies are similar. In the beginning they
are very difficult to control and the soul feels very
confined. Despite this, as you learn to control the body, the
feeling of restriction fades and you discover that you can
move in any way you want. The body gradually becomes
a part of you.

What is important to know is that like a bicycle, once
you know how to ride it, your body is very useful but if for
some reason, you are unable to control it, it can be highly
dangerous. It is like a child trying to ride an adult's
bicycle; it is so perilous and unstable that the child will not
be able to control it. It would be very hazardous if the
brakes did not work or the handlebars were bent. Much the
same can be said of the body.

What I am trying to say here is that people who are
able to maintain a good physical condition have taken the
first step toward victory in life. There are no two ways
about it. To a great extent, you are capable of mastering

health care on the personal level. It is like taking care of a bicycle, checking for bent handlebars, inefficient brakes or flat tires; if you are careful and look after it, you will be able to avoid all these things. If, when your bicycle has a puncture, you say, "Oh, it doesn't matter, it will be all right," you will find that you cannot use it when you most need it. The same is true of the brakes. You may think, "Oh, there are not many cars around, so I will be okay," but what will happen if a car suddenly pulls out in front of you? It is exactly the same with the body.

3) The Care of the Body Is Up to the Individual

As long as you maintain a healthy lifestyle, your physical body will work to accomplish its original purpose. If you do not look after your body you cannot blame others; you are the only person able to look after it. Managing your physical body is your own personal task.

An ex-officer in the Japanese Self-Defense Forces once told me how his soldiers went about parachute training. First the men practice jumping from a height of about fifty feet, next they jump off a tower about hundreds feet high, then they jump out of an airplane thousands feet above sea level and their parachutes open when they get down to a certain height. Each soldier looks after his own parachute. If it does not open, it could cost a man his life, so it is only natural not to entrust it to anyone else. If it does not open because of his own lack of care, then a man cannot blame anyone else. If, on the other hand, someone else had been responsible for its not opening, the soldiers would not be able to complain enough.

This example of the parachute may sound rather odd, but you are in a similar situation. To take the example of the parachute a little further, you could say that your soul is like the soldier and your body is the parachute. If the parachute were to rip or fail to open, it would be a tragedy; in the same way, if the body suffers a serious handicap or injury, it is a severe ordeal for the soul to overcome, regardless of whether it is foreseen or not.

At the very least, you should do everything you can to ensure that your body is kept out of danger. If you do not, the result is that your mind is affected negatively, and you have only yourself to blame. It makes no difference which dimension of the spirit world you are born from; even Angels of Light who have reincarnated become sick if they do not look after their bodies. It is an immutable law of this world. In the same way that a tire will get a puncture if a nail is been driven into it, the body will break down if it is not provided with a suitable amount of rest, nourishment and care.

If a professional baseball player were to be the opening pitcher every day, no matter how much he trained, he would not last more than a year at the most because pitchers usually need at least four days of rest between matches if they are to be able to continue their careers. This is quite easy to understand when talking about baseball players, but when it comes to the individual, most of us are scarcely aware of this.

It is very difficult to know how much you can work, how much rest you need and what you need to do to maintain your body in peak condition. It is not something you learn at school and, as with the mind, the maintenance of the body is left in the hands of the individual. Sometimes family members may help you stay in shape, but basically you have to do it on your own, without the help of others.

4) The Relationship between the Body and Mind
As people get older they tend to complain more. This is a common occurrence among those in their sixties or seventies who, at the same time, begin to worry about what might happen in the future and what has happened in the past. You may think that this is a problem of the mind, but why should it be that it affects people more when they get older? The main reason is that people find their bodies have become much weaker than they used to be.

As people age, their legs become weak and they are no longer able to get around as they once did. They become petulant, complaining constantly and the people around them find them increasingly difficult to live with. Eventually this can lead to problems within the family. The root of the problem is quite simple. After retirement, these people have not bothered to exercise their bodies, and this develops into a problem of the mind. But it is not just one person's problem; it involves the whole family and can become quite serious. Basically, after retirement people have fewer opportunities to use their bodies and often they have done nothing to compensate for this in other ways.

Younger people, too, often have problems that involve their bodies. There are some who eat too much and some who become so thin that they appear anorexic; in both cases, the reason is that they have forgotten how to lead a balanced life. There are those who love cakes and think that true happiness is eating two cakes a day. They cut down on other food and diet to avoid getting fat so it is hardly surprising they feel unwell. But in spite of this, they continue this behavior.

I understand how they feel, but I wish they would pull themselves together. If they are unable to stop, despite the fact that they have made themselves ill, then they have only themselves to blame for whatever happens next. People cannot live on cake alone; they need additional nutrients. The same is true of people who eat nothing but chocolate until their teeth rot. It is no one else's fault; they cannot lay the blame on God. The only person responsible for the fact that teeth are falling out is the person who ate too much chocolate.

So you need to take responsibility and look after your own body. This is particularly true of exercise. No one is going to tell you to get more exercise. No one will tell you how you should go about it, so you need to think of your body as something precious that has to be looked after, and engage in whatever exercise you feel is appropriate to the environment in which you live. The stronger your body, the stronger your mind becomes. If you are fit, you will feel positive, but if your body is weak, you will become increasingly pessimistic about everything.

So when you are feeling good, concentrate on positive thinking and when you are feeling bad, spend more time in self-reflection. Self-reflection is difficult when you are feeling euphoric or when you are running around in a state of elation, so at these times concentrate on positive thinking. Conversely, when you are slightly depressed, reflect on what you have done. Then you will become expert at utilizing both these techniques—I would like you to think about them, in addition to looking after your health.

3. The Creation of Wealth
1) Problems Connected to Having a Religious Disposition
The next theme I would like to discuss is the creation of wealth. There are a lot of people of a religious disposition who see money negatively, believing it is wrong for them to have wealth. This is true of followers of both Buddhism and Christianity.

The important point to consider here is that a person's level of poverty depends on the degree to which he or she feels wealth is wrong. Someone who believes strongly that possessing wealth will make it impossible for them to enter heaven will never become rich. If that is all they believe, it is not such a big problem. However, if they envy those who are rich and begin to criticize them, they will create hell in their own hearts. This is an example of the disharmony that self-constraint can create.

If you simply have no desire for money or other forms of luxury and have no attachment to them, then this could be considered a virtue. However, if you start to castigate those who are affluent and tell them their wealth will banish them to hell, a dark smog will begin to cover your mind and you will create an inner hell for yourself. It may seem strange but that is the way it works. Once you begin to bind yourself by exhibiting a tendency to criticize others, you had better watch out.

Another similar example is the problems created by the opposite sex. Money and the opposite sex are both subjects that are frequently misunderstood by people of a religious disposition. There are even people who believe that if they marry they will be barred from heaven, and those who want to believe that this will happen. I do not know which is more common, but such people actually do exist.

2) Wealth as a Means to Happiness

To find a solution to the problem posed by wealth, you have to ask yourself why wealth exists. "Wealth" can refer to money or to other assets, but why does it exist?

The reason wealth exists in this world is as a way of expressing the "richness" that exists in the Real World. The Real World is not a poor place. Wealth takes a variety

of forms and there is a law that states the pure in heart will
receive whatever they wish for. The inhabitants of the
Real World all live in purity so they are all prosperous.
However, the way in which wealth is expressed in the Real
World does not exist in the three-dimensional world, so
people try and use money as a substitute means of expression. Of course, wealth does not necessarily have to be
money, but money is a convenient form of expression.

The question is how money is used. In other words,
good and evil in relation to wealth in this world are
dependent on the motives and intentions of the user. For
instance, if an organization wants to build a hall it will
need money; if, by building the hall, it is able to hold
conferences and meetings that benefit people, then it is
money well-spent. They will also be able to rent the hall
out to others when they are not using it themselves, so
providing a facility. This is an example of how capital
creates space, and in so doing it furnishes people with
places to carry out activities that will bring joy and happiness. So, by creating space, money can be said to have
created happiness.

It is regrettable that wealth causes so many people
stumble. If we really want to help improve the world,
those who are pure in heart must teach others how to use
wealth correctly. We must also make sure that wealth is
created in the correct way. If this can be achieved, the
world will be a better place. I believe that wealth should
be channeled toward the construction of an ideal society

here on Earth. This is important, as wealth is the means of achieving happiness for a greater number of people.

3) Poverty Tainted by Envy Is Wrong

Here I would like to say that you cannot bend other people's principles. If you believe in purity through poverty, then no one will oppose you. If you wish to live your life according to that principle, then by all means go ahead; this is an acceptable way of living. However, if you do decide to live this way, you must also decide not to feel jealous of others. If you are content to live in honest poverty, then that is your decision as an individual, but you should never judge others. People all have different ways of living and different ways of thinking. When you elect to live in poverty, do not try to force others to do the same. Never express jealousy or envy—this is most important.

If your decision to live in honest poverty becomes tainted by envy, then poverty itself will be transformed into something negative. If, on the other hand, it allows you to get rid of attachment to material things, and the vibration of your mind is still pure, then poverty becomes a virtue. But if poverty leads to jealousy and envy of the material possessions of others, your heart will become clouded, and poverty can be considered wrong.

If you discover this negativity in yourself or in those around you, you need to fight to vanquish it. If you feel restricted by poverty, if it makes you feel miserable and envious of others, then you should make an effort to break out of it.

Some people worry because they have too much money, but compared to those who have no money or who are in debt, it can generally be said that they are in a much better position to find harmony in their hearts. It is often said that to have enough money to not have to worry is good, and basically I agree with this. Sufficient money to allow you to live without privation is a good thing. If you cannot admit this, your life will be one of envy and misery.

So if you want to live a life of honest poverty, do not envy others. If you cannot help being jealous, then make an effort to break out of poverty. It is important to set goals to create a certain amount of wealth, and then make the effort necessary to achieve them.

4) Three Basic Principles for the Creation of Wealth

There are three basic principles for the creation of wealth. The first principle, which has always been true, is thrift, that is to say economy, frugality and cutting out waste. This is the starting point. If you are wasteful or live an extravagant life, no matter how much money you may have, you will gradually use it all.

There is an old proverb that runs, "the third generation goes back to the mill." Someone from the first generation will work hard and take over the mill where he is employed, someone of the second generation will expand the business, someone of the third generation will cause the company to go bankrupt and go back to the mill and become a laborer. In most cases, this is because the third generation allow their lifestyle to become too grand and forget the hard work. As a result, they waste their money and soon find themselves ruined. This is true in both corporate and private life, and that is why I say that thrift—economy and frugality—are vitally important.

However, this is not to say you should become a miser. Unfortunately, misers never achieve real wealth either, so I am not recommending that you begrudge every penny you spend. I want you to avoid waste. It is important that you are moderate in your use of money so as not to waste the good fortune you have.

The second principle for the creation of wealth is that money accumulates around those who know how to use it. It will not suddenly appear in the middle of field, but it will come to those who know what it is for.

Huge sums of money accumulate in banks, and the reason for this is that banks are able to use this money to produce more. It is because they understand how to use it that the money comes to them. The same is true on a personal level; money will accumulate for those who know how to make use of it. For instance, if you decide that you want to build a house of your own, you will work harder to acquire the necessary finance. Or, if you have a lot of children and want to see them all through university, you will have to increase your earnings to achieve this.

In this way, money comes to people who know how to use it, so if you feel that you would like to be wealthier, it is important that first you have a clear idea of how you intend to use the money. You have to be able to say to yourself, "I need money for such and such a reason, so I want to be more prosperous." People who feel that they do not need money will never become rich. Even if they do succeed in acquiring a certain amount of wealth, it will only be on a limited scale. Real wealth only comes to those who have a clear idea of what they want the money for.

All over the world wealth is overflowing, looking for those who know how to use it. If these people appear, the money will automatically flow to them. In this, money can be said to resemble blood in a body; it flows to the places where it is needed most. There are a large number of people in the world who possess a lot of money but do not know how to use it. That is why when someone proposes a good idea about how to make use of money, wealth will automatically flow to them.

A good example of this is a new business. When people start a business, they find that the necessary capital will come together. Banks will invest in the business, as will partners; someone may appear and provide office space. So help comes from many different directions. It all begins with good ideas that move people's hearts; these attract energy from different places which, in turn, summon wealth. Wealth will gravitate to people with ideas and enthusiasm, in other words people who know how to use it. It is important to have lofty ideas about how to use wealth.

The third principle is the same as that of the "Laws of the Mind," which is "people who give will receive." If you succeed in gathering wealth, you should not try to monopolize it for yourself. Wealth will certainly circulate to you if you try and use it so as to contribute to improving the lifestyle of others and bringing them happiness. In other words, if you use your money just for your own sake, it will gradually disappear but if you try to use it for the sake of as many people as possible, you will find that it will continue to grow and multiply.

Let us look at the example of the work of the famous American automobile manufacturer, Henry Ford. In his lifetime, Henry Ford succeeded in amassing a huge fortune. The reason he was able to do this was that he dreamed of a time when everyone, even office employees and manual laborers, would be able to buy a car of their own. He wanted to build a car that people would be able to buy out of their own wages, with a single year's earnings, and gradually he was able to see his dream come true.

In Part One of this book, I talked about Konosuke Matsushita, the man who used to advocate what he called the "tap water philosophy." Although water is not free, there is such an inexhaustible supply that it appears to be. Even if a complete stranger stops and drinks from the tap in front of your house, you do not call him a thief or say that he has stolen your water. Water is not free, and he drinks it without your permission, so in the strictest sense of the law, he could be called a thief. But water is supplied at such a nominal cost that we think of it as being virtually free, so no one is going to call a man a thief for drinking it. Although he may have helped himself, no one is going to feel they have been robbed.

Mr. Matsushita's goal was to produce useful domestic electrical appliances cheaply, so people would think of them in the same way they think of water, and this was what he referred to as the "tap water philosophy." It is a form of the philosophy of love. As he hoped, his company succeeded in producing cheap electrical goods, and the result is that the current earnings are now hundreds of billions of yen per annum.

Love and wealth are given to those with a giving heart; they circulate and return to the giver, and accumulate to create even greater wealth. So to achieve infinite development, learning to share your wealth with others in the same way that you share love is essential. This is not to say that you should give your money to beggars; it is important that you use it so that it is able to be of service to others in many different ways.

There are numerous variations of methods of attaining wealth, but the three that I have described represent the basic methods. First, use your money with moderation; second, have a clear idea of how to use wealth, and third, be prepared to use what you have accumulated for the sake of others. If you follow these three principles, your wealth will not be considered wrong. As long as you observe these rules, your wealth will be a divine blessing. As you go about creating wealth, I would like you to bear this in mind, and remember that having greater influence through wealth is definitely not to be thought of as something negative.

4. Spouse and Home

1) Start by Making Yourself into Your Own Ideal

As the third theme, I want to consider the issue of spouses and the home. I would like to begin by looking at how to marry the ideal spouse. Some people worry about this for five, ten, even twenty years, but the answer is surprisingly simple. Contrary to what you probably expect, an ideal spouse is not someone you can find through pursuit; in fact, the harder you chase an ideal, the further you will move away from it.

I can almost hear you saying, "That cannot be true. You are always telling us that effort will be rewarded, and to those who ask shall be given. What do you mean, if we chase, the object will flee? That sounds very pessimistic." Of course, "those who ask shall be given" and "effort will be rewarded" are both truths, but in this section I am talking about marrying and the rules are somewhat different. Focusing on this, while it is true that if you have the will to marry you can achieve it, if you try hard and chase an ideal, you will be kept away from it.

This could be likened to dogs or cats chasing their own tails. You may have observed a puppy or kitten that has seen its own tail and tries to catch it, but no matter how hard it tries, it never succeeds. However, if it forgets about it and moves forward, the tail will follow. Finding a spouse is very much like this. People often refer to their spouse as their "better half," and it is in fact true that a spouse is like a part of yourself. If you chase an ideal, it will move away, but if you behave naturally and move forward, it will follow. This may sound strange, but it is a very apt metaphor.

What I would like to say here is first, you must make yourself into the kind of person your ideal spouse would want to marry. You may have various images of your ideal partner, but the first thing you need to do is to better yourself so that when the person of your dreams comes along, he or she will want to marry you.

The first priority should not be going out and searching for your ideal partner. Even if you make a list of all the characteristics you would look for in a spouse, saying, "This is my ideal, this is the kind of person I want to marry," then go and search for someone with them, unfortunately you will never find what you are looking for. Instead, you need to consider what kind of person your ideal partner would want to marry if he or she were to turn up. If you have set about making yourself into that person, then you will find your ideal partner will soon appear.

The reason I say this is that when you marry, it is important that both partners are an ideal match for one another. It is very important at this point that you match perfectly. This means that if you simply imagine your ideal partner and go in search of an ideal, you will not be able to find it. Unless you make yourself into the kind of person who is the right match, even if you do meet, the other person will simply pass you by, like an express train speeding through a station.

It is okay to search for an ideal and carry that image in your mind, but first you must think about how you would appear if you were ever to meet your ideal. Suppose you had a crush on a famous film star and went to see him or her make a speech. What would you do if that person talked to you and put their arm round your shoulders? It is very likely you would run away, and you would never be able to marry your ideal if you behaved like that. If you run away out of fear or embarrassment, you will never get close. You must work on yourself so that when you do meet that person, he or she will think that you are the ideal partner. This is a very important point.

For young people especially, it is vital that you establish yourself in a career, because you will achieve what is most important through your work. As well as the prospect of financial success, it is extremely important that young people have a clear vision of their future.

There are a lot of people who, despite the fact that they are introduced to numerous prospective partners, are unable to marry. This kind of person will most likely say they cannot find anyone they like, or they cannot find an ideal partner. In actual fact, the problem is that they are unable to assess themselves objectively. As a result of this inability to look at themselves objectively, they are unable to say what kind of person would make a suitable partner. They keep raising and lowering their sights, trying hard to find someone to be with, but in the end they cannot find anyone.

However, if they were able to say exactly what their own future prospects were, they would soon discover someone who suited them. It does not matter whether they work for a company or start their own business; they must be able to say, "I work for such and such a company, my future will develop in such and such a way, and I will earn this much money in the future." If they are able to do this and are enthusiastic, they are sure to find a suitable partner.

If you think that your job is boring and you want to leave as soon as possible, I am afraid that no matter how many people you are introduced to, you will never find the ideal partner. Again, if you tell yourself you want to leave your present position, but you are waiting until you have tied the knot so as not to spoil your chances of marriage, I am afraid you will not find the right person. It is very strange, but that is the way life works.

Whether you arc a man or woman, what it boils down to in the end is that you have to make yourself into the kind of person your ideal partner would want to be with. This is what is most important.

2) Can You Achieve a Deep Understanding of Your Partner?

The second point I would like to discuss in this context, the most important prerequisite if you intend to marry, regardless of whether you are a man or a woman, which is that you are capable of understanding your partner. There are lots of other conditions that have to be met, but this one has top priority.

You may worry about appearance, whether someone is attractive or ugly, tall or short, fat or thin, whether he or she has a lot of money or a good scholastic record. There are all sorts of factors to choose from and, as a result, many people do not know which to place most emphasis on. A person may be clever but poor, handsome but short, beautiful but stupid, so people cannot make up their minds about which criteria are most important. You could try asking others for advice, but you will probably end up even more confused than before.

One person may say that looks are most important, another that you should not worry about appearance but concentrate on a person's disposition, a third may remark that intelligence is the thing to look for, while a fourth may insist that a good background is vital. It is very difficult to decide, and I am sorry to have to say that you will never come across a person who meets all your conditions. You will have to accept someone who has one or two short-comings, so the question has to be where you place your priorities.

To talk in generalities, what is most important is to look for someone you can understand. It does not matter how much money a person has, because once it has all been used up there will be nothing left between you. Although a person may be very good-looking, the attraction will fade as you see them every day. Although you may want to marry someone because they have a great personality, one day you will realize that they also have faults.

All that leaves is a deep mutual understanding. A good mutual understanding is something that will continue for twenty, thirty, even forty years, whereas if you look only at external or objective characteristics, although you may get on well when you first marry, the rapport between you will gradually break down and cracks will appear in the relationship.

Suppose a woman thinks that academic status is the most important characteristic in a man, and marries someone who has graduated from one of the top universities. Although he may have studied hard when he was young, after leaving university he may have become very fond of drinking, staying out every night from Monday to Friday, and coming home late with his face as red as a beet. She may have married him because he went to an elite university, but if he drinks till his whole body turns red, is never without a drink and even drinks in the morning before he goes to the office, she is bound to be disappointed. Sometimes people change after marriage.

Perhaps this woman married him because she thought he was intelligent; unfortunately, however, intelligence and academic achievement are not always the same. Truly intellectual people do not necessarily do well in school. While there is some correlation between intelligence and scholastic ability, it is not one hundred percent; in fact, I would say that in most cases, the correlation is about sixty to seventy percent.

This variation comes about as a result of individual inclinations. For instance, someone with an intellectual bent will become increasingly intellectual, despite the fact that the person may not even have been to high school. As these sorts of people grow older, by thirty or forty years of age, they have gradually turned into genuine intellectuals, whereas someone who was forced to study as a child may grow up to detest it. Although the person who was forced to study may actually be a very clever individual, he may end up like the person in the example I gave just now, coming home drunk every night and throwing away a career. Although he may have been highly intelligent at twenty-two or twenty-three, by the time he reaches forty, he has become a completely different person.

There are various factors on which to base the decision to marry, but if you are going to take just one, then you should look at how well you can understand the other person. Ask yourself if you have a deep understanding of your partner, whether you can understand his or her outlook on life. If you feel that you can see through to the depths of his or her character, then the chances are that you will have a happy married life.

Ask yourself how far your prospective partner is capable of understanding your thoughts on work or life. Is your partner capable of only a shallow appreciation, or does your partner possess deep insight into the way you think? If you feel strongly that he or she can understand you, and that this understanding is mutual, then it is probably safe to go ahead and marry.

In this section, I have described two ways of finding the ideal spouse. The first is not to chase the person you wish to marry, rather to alter yourself to fit the other person's ideal. Secondly, I stressed the importance of understanding. Whether or not you have the ability to understand a prospective spouse and whether he or she can understand you is very important.

3) You Need to Work to Make a Perfect Match

Next, I would like to touch on how to sustain a relationship after marriage. Although a couple may be happy in the period immediately following their marriage, there are people whose relationships gradually break down, which leads to separations.

The people who are most likely to suffer this kind of outcome are those who believe that men and women are like a lock and key, that each must match the other perfectly. They believe that if they marry a certain type of person, they will be able to achieve happiness, but if they do not, the marriage will end in acrimony. People who see others in this way as some kind of object will often find that their marriages end in failure. They may have thought they could find true happiness if they married person A, whereas if they married person B, they would not. If they feel that things did not work out because they ended up marrying B, it is hardly surprising that their marriage has not lasted.

An ideal match between people is something that has to be worked on; it is not something that just happens, allowing people to live happily ever after. If a couple feel they get along to a certain extent, after that they have to work at their relationship to make it a perfect match. This means that before you say your partner does not suit you, you need to ask yourself if there is something that you could do, some idea that you have not thought of, some effort that is lacking in you.

Both a man and a woman must make every effort to understand their partner. Please try and act in this way. Actually there are not many people you cannot get on with at all. Once you have reached a certain stage, it is simply a matter of effort. You may have numerous crises in your relationship, but when they threaten to destroy it, you must be inventive and ingenious in finding a way to overcome them. This willingness to make an effort is something I hope you will not forget.

5. Encounters That Will Change Your Destiny

1) Expect to Encounter a "Noble" Person

The fourth theme I would like to talk about is fateful encounters. My readers are all of different ages, and if you are around twenty years old you have probably only met one or two people who have changed your life; in fact, you may have yet to meet any. However, as you get older and reach thirty, forty or fifty, you will encounter people who have a hand in changing your life.

If you look back over your life, you will notice several major turning points; at each of them was someone who had an influence on your destiny. Whenever you look at this kind of turning point, you will always find a person who affected you in some way. Whenever you come to a junction in your life and have to decide whether to turn left, turn right or go straight ahead, you are sure to find someone standing there to help you. In many cases, your destiny changes according to how you handle the encounter with this person.

Of course, what you want at such times is someone who will change your destiny for the better, but sometimes the opposite happens. There are people who discover that as the result of a chance meeting, their lives take a sharp turn for the worse. Perhaps they are cheated or go into business with someone only to find themselves bankrupt. Perhaps a teacher at school gives some advice which, when followed, leads to disaster. Although this kind of thing can happen, the kind of encounter I would like to consider here is the positive one. To succeed in life, it is important that you treasure meetings with people who can lead you to happiness and good fortune.

In China there is the concept of a "noble" person and a common greeting in that country is "Have you met a noble person recently?" In most cases, the expression refers to someone with integrity, someone of a higher rank, better educated or richer than you, and at the very least in a position to help you better yourself. I have heard this greeting is frequently used in daily life, in the same way as we enquire about someone's health or current situation. An encounter with a "noble" person is of great significance.

At Happy Science, we stress the importance of individual effort and self-discipline, but these can both be likened to a staircase you can only progress up one step at a time. On the other hand, the appearance of a "noble" person can be compared to an elevator. Once you get into the elevator, you can travel a number of stories almost instantaneously, and when you get out you will find yourself in a completely different world from the one you have just left. This is something that happens several times in the course of a life.

To put it another way, everyone meets people who usher in good luck. I am sure you have experienced an encounter with someone who has changed your life completely. It is very true that at every turning point in your life there is someone who says something, maybe

without much thought or not very seriously, and this later
acts as an important guide for you. The person in question
may have forgotten the incident, but this definitely
happens.

So, there are times when someone appears and offers
you the key to better fortune and when they do, it is important that you listen to their advice or opinion, and move in
the right direction. It is impossible to say just when this
person will appear before you, because the timing of this
encounter differs from person to person, but you should
always be ready to make the most of a meeting with
someone who will guide you. If you wish for this sort of
encounter, you can be sure that the person will appear.

When you do come across this person, your life will
begin to radiate light, and no matter who you are, you can
be quite sure that there will be this sort of dazzling time at
some point in the course of your life. People who say that
they have never experienced this are probably ungrateful,
or have forgotten. It comes in many forms, so please think
carefully about this, as it really will provide you with the
key to a great step forward.

The more you have prepared yourself for this kind of
encounter, the greater the likelihood of it happening. So
every year, hold yourself in readiness and expect that
someone will offer you advice that will lead you in a better
direction and open up a bright future, because if you do,
this sort of person will always appear. If you hold yourself
in readiness for this sort of encounter every month, then

the right person will appear before you on a monthly basis.
The possibility of these meetings occurring depends on
how strongly you anticipate them.

The reason for this is that if you constantly anticipate
these sorts of encounters, it will spur your guardian spirit
or other guiding spirits to cause one to come about. They
begin to think you should be rewarded for sustaining such
a laudable attitude and they go about finding someone
who will be able to help you get ahead. You may actually
come to a turning point in your life through meeting this
sort of person directly, or it may happen through the
agency of your guardian spirit without your realizing.
However, either way, something will definitely happen.

People are always watching you. They see you on
different occasions and many of them would like to do
something to help you get ahead. The first prerequisite for
meeting this kind of person is the earnest desire for this
sort of encounter.

2) Listen Humbly to What You Are Told

The second prerequisite for fateful encounters is humility.
It is important that you admit to yourself there are many
people in this world who are wiser than you, and when
you meet one of them, you need to listen humbly to what
they say. If you fail to listen, you will miss your opportunity. You should always be on the lookout for words that
might lead you to change yourself and expect encounters
with people who make crucial comments.

Next, you should make sure that you do not miss what they say, so that you do not waste a valuable encounter. When you feel, "This is the goddess of happiness, the goddess of good fortune," do not let it pass you by, but make the most of the chance that is being offered. This kind of fateful meeting is one of the most important events of your life. It really is a shining moment, so I would like you to take it seriously. It is a time when you are standing at the crossroads of destiny, and all kinds of people will offer their assistance to allow you to change your life. If you believe that you have achieved what you have solely through your own efforts, you are quite mistaken. It is impossible to achieve anything by yourself, so I would like you to remain humble and do not forget to listen to what these people tell you.

As this part is entitled "Life and Victory," you may have been expecting to hear about achievement through one's own efforts, but contrary to your expectations, the way to true victory lies in a helping hand from others. Opportunities are offered by many. If a lot of people are trying to help you further your career, it is quite difficult not to succeed. If, on the other hand, a lot of people are trying to stop you from succeeding, it becomes very difficult to get ahead and requires an immense effort. If others want to help you, you can be successful simply by going with the flow. This is something you need to be grateful for.

To sum up, people do not achieve success by their own efforts alone. It is important always to remember that it is through the help of others that you are able to achieve your goals.

3) Have a Grateful Heart

I would be lying if I were to say that it did not take a lot of effort to get to where I am now, but the reason I was able to walk the path I did is because I received the support of a large number of people on Earth, as well as help from heaven.

In the usual terms, I suppose this could be described as "luck," but for someone like me who knows about the existence of the Real World firsthand, it is impossible to use the word "luck." I know that it is a result of the cooperation of those who reside in the other world, and it is through their very real work that I have been blessed with such good fortune. This feeling of gratitude is very important. When your fortunes take a turn for the better, do not forget to express your gratitude.

If you are to be blessed by an upturn in fortune, it is important to remember three points. First, always seek earnestly and anticipate a change in your fortunes. Second, remain humble and listen to advice. Third, always have gratitude in your heart. If you follow these rules, I believe that when you reach a turning point in life, it will be one that truly radiates light.

6. A Spiritual Legacy

1) Integrity as a Spiritual Legacy

For the fifth and final theme, I would like to discuss the subject of a spiritual legacy. In the first section, I discussed how to live a healthy life, in the second, I considered the creation of wealth, in the third, the spouse and home, and in the fourth I talked about encounters that can change your destiny (fateful encounters). Depending on the way in which you read them, they may create the impression of a guide to material success, or an explanation of how to get ahead in this world.

However, this part is entitled "Life and Victory," and it is impossible to discuss this fully without considering what is beyond mere worldly success. It is vital that you go beyond earthly success. Unless you possess that which surpasses earthly success, you cannot claim to have achieved true victory in life.

What is it that transcends worldly success? I always teach of "a happiness that continues both in this world and the next," a form of happiness that you can take with you when you die. What form does this happiness take? It is very spiritual, and can be described as a treasure of the heart, that is not of this world.

In other words, to those who have come into contact with and understood the Laws of the Truth, victory in life means more than just worldly success. It would be no exaggeration to say that unless you have grasped something greater, a spiritual legacy, it cannot be said that you have been victorious in life. I have introduced this idea in numerous books before and you have perhaps already studied it. However, I would like to run through it once more with you.

"A spiritual legacy" is a very abstract-sounding phrase, but if I were to give it another name, I could call it integrity. Ability is something that you are born with; its seeds are there from the day you arrive in this world. Even if you do not cultivate them, the potential is there and it is left to you to develop. Integrity, however, is something you do not possess when you are born. It is something that comes into being in the course of your life here in the three-dimensional world, it is an acquired trait. Of course, it goes without saying that the high spirits of the Real World, for example, the Angels of Light in the seventh dimension possess integrity, but even they are not endowed with it when they are born into this world. However, they do have abilities. You are born with abilities, but not with integrity.

2) *Two Ways That Integrity Comes into Being*
So how do you acquire integrity? It develops gradually over a period of several decades, but do you have any idea how it comes into being?

There are two sorts of circumstances through which integrity can be acquired. One is in the midst of discouragement, failure and adversity; the other is through success. These are the times when integrity can be most easily attained. Of course, integrity can be achieved to a lesser extent at other times in your life, but great integrity, which stands as a memorial to your life, comes into being through these two experiences.

Let us think about why integrity comes into existence at times when we feel discouraged, disappointed or face adversity. It is quite usual to complain about bad luck when suffering adversity, but as you may know there are some people who do not just grumble and bemoan their misfortune. Most people, when they make a mistake, blame luck or their circumstances at the time. They may accuse others of letting them down or even blame their guardian spirits, but most cannot stand the pressures adversity and discouragement bring.

Others who have achieved a slightly higher state of consciousness will not allow themselves to be crushed by adversity but try to accept it for what it is, enduring it. People who try to bear their misfortune in this way are better than the average. Above these stand the people who make the effort to live optimistic, happy lives, despite adversity. These people can be said to stand on the bottom rungs of a higher level of consciousness.

However, the people who are really to be admired are those who use invincible thinking to counteract all adversity. When faced with misfortune, they are able to detect a divine intention in it and ask themselves what this affliction is supposed to teach them. They are sure to learn the lesson from their setback. They read the divine intention in their predicament and ask themselves what it is that they need, what this adversity is trying to teach them, and use this as the basis upon which to build their character or as a principle underpinning their actions. People who experience this develop integrity. They possess an extraordinary strength that radiates light.

To be able to endure difficulties or disappointment is in itself remarkable, but really extraordinary people read the divine intention in their experience, search within it for some seed that will lead them to success, and then nurture that seed. To be able to achieve this is truly extraordinary, and here integrity comes into being.

The second sort of circumstances that give rise to integrity involve success. People whose names go down in history are those who have experienced success in their lives. No matter how many times they may have failed, in the end they achieved great success. Take Abraham Lincoln, for example. He was defeated in elections, his personal relationships failed, and he suffered a succession of hardships including his fiancée's death, but finally he became the President of the United States and left behind great achievements. Had he not become President, he would not be remembered as a great historical figure to this day. In the end he did achieve success.

Even if you experience a succession of setbacks, you will eventually have the chance to bloom. When success finally comes, the way you handle it is very important. You must not try to claim the fruits of success for yourself.

Rather, tell yourself that it was not achieved by your own efforts, but by the will of heaven. Although you may have supplied the water and fertilizer while it was still embryonic in form, you did not bring it about by yourself. The flower of success was already present inside the seed when it was offered to you, and it blossomed of its own accord. You simply helped it on its way, supplying it with water and nourishment. This is how you should regard it.

Do not take the credit yourself; rather, consider that although you may have assisted it to a certain extent, it came about through the will of heaven. The attitude of not trying to turn success into a personal achievement gives rise to great integrity. If you take all the credit yourself and believe your success came about solely as the result of your own efforts and skills, you will never develop integrity; it is merely the experience of achieving success through your own abilities.

What will happen if you do not attempt to take the credit for success, if you say that it was the result of the efforts of numerous people? What if you believe that your success is the will of heaven, that it came about as a result of the wishes of your guardian and guiding spirits? If you think that success is a result of the will of God, how will you act? You will certainly try to ensure that your success benefits the greatest number of people, and this is how integrity develops.

Each person leads a different life, but integrity arises from these two causes regardless. It is something that has to be attained so I would like you to strive to attain some measure of integrity, no matter how little, so that you can take it with you as a spiritual legacy when you return to the other world. Only then will you be able to say that you have truly achieved victory in life. I hope that you will be able to experience it in this lifetime.

PART FOUR

The Power of Invincible Thinking

4: The Power of Invincible Thinking

1. A Theory That Links Self-Reflection and Progress
At Happy Science, I introduce the Fourfold Path—love, wisdom, self-reflection and progress—as principles of happiness. The theme of this book, "invincible thinking," is a philosophy that links self-reflection and progress. Generally, when people practice positive thinking, they tend to think it is sufficient simply to move forward in a positive and constructive manner. However, we need to consider how to reconcile this with self-reflection, one of my basic teachings.

If people are told to reflect on their thoughts and deeds one day, and urged to move forward using positive thinking the next, some will waver between the two, not knowing which to concentrate upon. Until now, I have left it up to the individual to decide which method to adopt, and this may have caused some confusion. For this reason, I have introduced the idea of invincible thinking as a way of connecting these two ideas, and making the theory

clearer. I would like you to use invincible thinking when
you have no idea how to solve a problem, because it is an
effective philosophy that includes both self-reflection and
progress.

When practicing positive thinking, people tend not to
look into the shadows, not to look at the dark side of
things. They only look to the light, focusing on the bright
side of things, or look at things only in a constructive
way. While this philosophy is very powerful, if you focus
only on this direction, it leaves no room for self-reflection. But no matter how positive and forward-looking you
may be, there are times when things do not go smoothly.
I am sure you have experienced failure in the past. Is it
really all right on such occasions to ignore it and advance
regardless?

You have probably told yourself that everything would
be all right as long as you kept on moving forward, as long
as you maintained a positive attitude. Even if you fell or
made mistakes, you probably said, "I don't worry about
things like this, I just remain in the light. After all, a
person's nature is essentially light." Those who practice
positive thinking tend to think like this, but is this really
all there is to life? Are people's feelings really that simple?

Having studied the hearts and minds of human beings,
I was forced to ask myself if this really was enough. Is it
sufficient for people to advance in just one direction,
following just one pattern of thinking? No, of course not.
People's hearts and minds are full of deep feelings and

thoughts, so surely there needs to be a deep philosophy to take account of these.

2. The Power of Invincible Thinking
   ## in the Phenomenal World

Invincible thinking is a personal philosophy unique to each and every individual. Despite this, I strongly feel that I need to offer an explanation of the direction and approach you should take, so here I would like to discuss the power of invincible thinking from this perspective.

This philosophy started from the idea that no one can live without making mistakes. No one is capable of sailing through life without any problems. The reality is that people move to the left then to the right, they fail and go down, then they stand up again, but always they are searching for some way to make their lives better and happier. In the face of this reality, what is needed to lead a successful life? This is what I would like to consider now.

Invincible thinking is a philosophy that provides you with the greatest power that exists in the three-dimensional world you inhabit, this world where you breathe and eat. Of course, there are principles that go beyond the three-dimensional world, for instance, one of the laws of self-realization is the Law of Will.

In the Real World, you can manifest almost one hundred percent of your innate power but this is not necessarily the case in this three-dimensional world. Each person is capable of manifesting to a different extent. The monism of Light which states "there is essentially only light" becomes more effective in the higher dimensions, but here in the three-dimensional world, it does not necessarily apply. Invincible thinking explains spiritual laws that are not fully understood, especially from the standpoint of this phenomenal world.

3. Transform Difficulties into Strength for Your Soul
I would like to start by saying that invincible thinking is based on the idea that all difficulties in life can be turned into nourishment for the soul. You will probably face various setbacks, failures and difficulties during the course of your life, but seen from the perspective of your purpose in coming to this world, should you simply try to avoid them? This is something that I would like you to think about. Were you really born just to avoid the difficulties and hardships that arise? This is a question you must answer.

When you think about the meaning of life, you will realize it is not the case. You are born here on this Earth once every few hundred or few thousand years so that you may work with many types of people in new circumstances to refine your soul further. Life on this Earth is not necessarily filled with good experiences, but before you were born, you all knew this.

You are not here simply to have everything run smoothly for you. Your purpose on Earth is to develop greater stature and radiate a genuine light by accumulating many different experiences, repeating the process of trial and error. If you look at the purpose of your life in this way, what you thought of as difficulties and hardships will take on a new meaning. This realization is the basis of invincible thinking.

If you base your thinking on the fact that human beings have eternal life and return to Earth repeatedly through the process of reincarnation, you will be able to look at all the events and experiences of this phenomenal world from a different perspective and see that these experiences are provided to supply your inner being with invaluable nourishment. This is the basis of invincible thinking.

The main challenge in life is how to make the utmost effort, using all the knowledge, skills and ideas you possess, to cope with the problems you are confronted with and transform what you gain into strength for your soul. So, never be satisfied simply to avoid or deny a problem. This is expressed in my teaching that states, "Life is like a workbook to be problems to be solved, and one must make the effort to solve each problem."

You have your own workbook of problems to be solved, and you have to answer them all by yourself. This is something I want you to think of as a prerequisite for learning invincible thinking. You must solve your own problems yourself, and once you have done so, or even while you are in the throes of doing so, think about guiding others. Then, do not be satisfied just to help others, but also work to establish some large, positive undertaking. This is the framework of invincible thinking.

4. Be Master of Your Own Time

I would now like to look at the sort of thinking that is important if you are to gain real power from invincible thinking. Basically, it could be summed up as having an indomitable spirit.

Since founding Happy Science, I have come into contact with a large number of people and heard about many different ways of thinking. Some people seem to live in the light, others in the dark; some are buoyant, others depressed, and all seem to be going through a variety of small, personal dramas. As a result of coming into contact with the activities of our organization, many were able to change their lives.

In the course of a life, people experience many different periods, of light and dark, of happiness and depression, times when things go their way and times when they do not. If people were to be observed in such circumstances and classified according to the way they reacted, everyone would fall into one of the following two groups.

One type is the people who do extremely well when things are going their way, when they have a tail wind and everything seems to be working out for them, but as soon as they run into a head wind, they cannot cope. Although they sail swiftly along when they have a good wind in their sails, as soon as the wind swings round and changes direction, they find they cannot move forward; some of them even capsize. The vast number of people fit into this category.

The other type is the people who have an indomitable spirit. They demonstrate a strong, pure will that was with them from the outset and they constantly show a tenacity. A person's will can be very powerful at certain times, but whether or not it is genuine is tested by the passage of time.

Invincible thinking is a philosophy that allows you to be master of your own time, and to keep time under your control. To see whether you have assimilated this philosophy, you need to think back to how you were six months ago, for instance, or a year or two, or three years ago. Looking at what you have achieved in this time, have you gone forward or backward, strayed or continued on the right path? You always need to check on your own course in this way. If you look back over the path you have been taking and find you have made progress on a single, steady path, it means that although you may have suffered losses in some small instances, on the whole, you have continued to win the big match.

So invincible thinking is like the growth of a tree. As it grows, a tree is faced with numerous challenges and hardships. Strong winds may blow and strip the branches of their leaves. The tree may come close to dying, it may lack nourishment, or its roots may be exposed. However, no matter what happens, it struggles to keep growing ever taller. Invincible thinking is based on this kind of effort.

5. The Energy of Bamboo That Creates Joints

To use a different metaphor, I would like you to think about bamboo. Perhaps you have admired the bamboo plant when you have seen it growing, and looking at a stem, its joints tapering to the top, you probably thought of the joints simply as a kind of pattern. However, when I look at it, I wonder what makes bamboo put so much effort into creating joints.

The joints of bamboo occur at intervals of eight to twelve inches, and each joint is very strong. At the base, the joints are bigger and stronger, and they become increasingly smaller and weaker toward the top, bending in the wind. However, over time, the thin, weak parts grow stronger to become large joints, and the top grows still higher. If you look at bamboo, you can see it grows steadily, segment by segment. I find it very impressive. Whether it grows to a height of thirty feet or sixty feet, what makes it unique and the reason that bamboo is bamboo is its joints.

Bamboo is resistant to wind. No matter how strong the wind, bamboo will not break easily. It is not a strong plant, but you can tell that it is certainly not weak either by the fact that it is so resilient. The wind may blow, the rain may fall, but it just keeps on growing regardless. It marks the growth on its stem for you to see, as if saying, "This is how much I have grown." I have pondered how the bamboo must feel as it creates these joints. As each one is added, it must think to itself, "I have managed to grow this much taller," and I am sure this must give it a sense of accomplishment.

The way in which you construct your life in many ways resembles the bamboo. You are just like the bamboo which remains thin. Even the biggest bamboo stalk is only eight to ten inches across; they cannot grow any bigger. The bamboo first appears above the ground as a shoot, then it grows steadily. It does not lose its initial flexibility, neither does it lose its strength. Flexibility and strength exist together in harmony, and this is what is needed for growth.

In other words, what I call "invincible thinking" is a philosophy that allows you to grow through both the good and the bad times in life, and in this, it is like the growth of the bamboo. Basically, bamboo is flexible, flexible yet strong. It is not sufficient for it to be able to bend in just one direction, or not bend at all. Persimmon trees do not sway or bend like bamboo, and they break quite easily. Bamboo does not snap, but persimmon trees do. As you know, willows do not break easily either. Something that looks sturdy can actually be quite weak and snap easily. However, what is flexible has the real strength within and is hard to break. This is what you should aim for, because the three-dimensional world in which you are living is not some kind of greenhouse; it is a world where rain falls, winds blow, and there are snowstorms and periods of drought.

I have used bamboo as a metaphor, but come to think of it, both your life and fate seem to go in cycles. I cannot say how long each cycle lasts, it may be several years or several months, but one thing is certain—there are times when everything goes well and times when things do not run smoothly. I believe that it is in the times of adversity that what is truly wonderful is born. At the turning points in your life, inevitably you experience a lack of harmony with your environment and the people around you, and you suffer. But if I were asked whether it would be better for you not to have to go through these times, I would have to say no, because these times of hardship are when marvelous things begin.

Looking at life in this way, you will realize that there is no need to fear adversity. In times of adversity, your soul receives the greatest nourishment and you are able to learn the most important lessons. This can be likened to the time when bamboo makes a new joint. It grows eight to twelve inches steadily, until it reaches the point where it needs to create a joint. I imagine this must be a painful time for the bamboo. It probably wishes it could just continue growing smoothly in the same way it has been up to that time, without making a joint. It may dream of how wonderful it would be to grow thirty or even sixty feet without interruption. However, it has to stop every eight to twelve inches to create a joint. I am sure it must experience a feeling of resistance and stagnation when this happens; it must wonder why it is no longer able to grow as it pleases, why it has to suffer such an interruption.

It must be a painful time for the bamboo, because although it wants to continue growing, it has to produce a joint. I imagine it suffers confusion, feeling as if it has come up against a barrier, but soon the energy wells up inside and the joint is created. Once the joint is formed, the bamboo can grow normally again until it is time to make another one. The process of creating these joints may be very painful for the plant, but it is on account of these that it is able to keep growing continuously, although it may not realize it. The joints provide the basis for its growth.

What it comes down to is that fate and luck run in cycles. There are times when things go well and times when nothing works out, times of opportunity and times of adversity, which are the periods when you grow and produce joints. Times of adversity are the joints in your life, and after you have created a joint, you can advance to the next step.

I would like you to look back over your past and consider when you were able to learn most. I am sure that you have suffered at some time; you may have been hurt by the words of others, you may have had difficulties in business, gone bankrupt or suffered illness. However, after an interval of five or ten years, looking back on these experiences, you realize that these were the times that provided you with your sweetest memories. So when you find life unbearable, tell yourself that you are in the middle of creating a joint before you move forward to the next stage on the path of growth.

6. Creating Annual Rings in a Harsh Environment

In the last section, I used the growth of bamboo as a metaphor for life, but an ordinary tree would serve just as well. Unlike bamboo, trees do not have joints but they do have annual rings.

When I lived in the country, I built an incinerator for burning rubbish. It was a simple affair of bricks and stones to keep the fire from spreading. Standing nearby was a tree and I thought the heat of the fire would kill it. However, contrary to my expectations it did not; in fact, it became much tougher than before and although other trees died, this one continued to grow.

Life must have been very harsh for that tree growing right next to the incinerator, but its growth during that period was marked by annual rings. Its trunk grew progressively thicker and it was full of life force. Strangely enough, I saw trees that were growing in more hospitable places which were quickly blown over in typhoons. If we compare this to human life, it could be said that the other trees were like the so-called elite, who work for the large corporations. They come from wealthy backgrounds and have lived their whole lives without ever experiencing hardship, but as soon as a gale blows, that is to say as soon as they suffer some setback in their career, they are unable to withstand the pressure.

On the other hand, those who have been brought up in tough conditions and who possess a strength that has been forged by hardship do not give in so easily. Strong in the face of adversity, they are able to get through any difficulty, and so they are able to overcome all kinds of obstacles, marking up annual rings in their characters to increase their stature.

If you read the biographies of great people, you will notice that in many cases they have lived through hard times. This illustrates how without experiencing such adverse conditions they would not have been able to mark up the annual rings on their souls. So it is vital to endure difficult situations in the course of a life. As for myself, I am able to stand before people and give them advice on life's problems because I too have lived through some difficult times. What I have given thought to in those periods has been converted to strength.

When your body and soul are faced with the buffeting winds of misfortune, and the heat and snow of tribulation, your soul develops the power to resist any misfortune, and it is like an immunity. As a result, you come to understand how to overcome life's problems. Once you have this expertise, you are able to check new knowledge and others' experiences against your own, and come up with new ideas. In the end, every experience you have accumulated becomes a lesson, which is converted into a powerful energy for your soul.

7. Think Like a Long-Distance Runner

So far, this part of the book has been about indomitable spirit, and now I would like to consider a related subject, short-term and long-term thinking. There are two ways of considering a situation, in the short term and in the long term.

You should not consider things only in the long term, and deem the present unimportant. It is not good to say, "I will stock up on provisions in winter, so I can do whatever I want now." Although it may be summer, there are still things to do. You should not pass the days indolently, thinking just because you have laid in enough wood and coal to see you through the winter, you have nothing more to worry about. You must do all that is necessary in each season.

However, just when you feel like giving up and think that things could not possibly get worse, that you could not endure any further hardship or privation, I would like you to bear in mind that such periods in your life are generally very brief. If you focus on just one or two short years, you may feel depressed that things have not gone as you would have liked, but at such times you need to change your way of thinking completely.

The fact that you did not succeed in the short term may mean that you do not have the potential to be a sprinter. You may not be able to win the hundred yard dash, but this does not necessarily mean that you do not have any ability to be a runner. There are the sprints over a few hundred yards and there are marathons which last twenty-six miles. If you are no good at sprinting, then ask yourself whether you have any talent for long-distance running. Sometimes, I would like you to change your perspective.

I myself have never been a very good runner, but when I was in senior high school, I once took part in a marathon and achieved quite a satisfactory position. This experience of long-distance running taught me the importance of pacing myself in all things. When the race started, I chose a group of people who I felt were of about the same ability as me and I ran with them to pace myself. However, after I had been running for a while, my body warmed up, I felt good and realized that I might be able to do better than I had originally expected. From about the halfway point, I began to increase my pace and it felt as if my legs had grown longer. I was able to continue increasing my speed until I found myself overtaking people who had always beaten me in sprints.

Sprinters are usually well-built and if they get the pace wrong in a long-distance race, they find that they cannot keep going. If they run too fast, they drop out halfway, panting and pausing for rest. I could see the amazement on the sprinters' faces as I overtook them and although they made an effort to stay ahead, they could not keep up and dropped behind. I could hardly believe it was happening, it was indeed an amazing experience.

I have talked here about the importance of pacing yourself. You need to assess your own strength objectively and decide when you should make extra effort so that you can achieve the best possible result in the long run. There is always room for improvement.

8. The Cumulative Effect

I imagine that for some of the members of Happy Science, studying the Truth is a real headache. Perhaps they worry that they do not have the time to study the books of Truth or they have difficulty learning at seminars.

If you look only at the short term, it is true that people have different levels of ability. For instance, if a group of people is asked to master something over the course of a year, some will manage this much faster than others. However, the objective is not to achieve a high level of awareness in a single year, nor to leave this world within one year. The challenge is how much nourishment you can acquire for your soul in this lifetime, how much you are able to improve your character before you return to the Real World.

If you rush in and try to achieve something in the short term, there is a good chance you will not succeed. However, if you look at the long term, you will realize that there are many other ways of thinking about things. It is pointless to cut time up into one-year segments so as to measure someone's achievements or ability. It may not even be enough to limit a segment to three or four years. It is necessary to extend the time frame. If some people tire of a subject after a year or two and give up, you should tell yourself you will continue studying longer. This is how you should change your thinking.

If you do this, you will be thinking like a long-distance runner and gradually, you will see positive results. Strangely enough, contrary to expectations, you will find yourself achieving results very quickly, almost as if you were a sprinter. The reason you are able to do this is the result of the cumulative effect, an accumulative effect. Although you may not possess any particular ability and curse yourself for your slowness, if you continue to make an effort, you will find that a cumulative effect will begin to work. After you have attained a certain degree of discipline and accumulated a certain stock of knowledge, you will find what used to take a long time in the past can be achieved ever more speedily. It seems strange but that is the way it works.

If you mix yeast and rice, and leave them to stand, they will ferment to produce sake. In the same way, if you store experiences, you will find that after a certain period of time they come to fruition. This will happen when you least expect it and provide the power to propel you forward. However, I should warn you that this fermentation takes a number of years to occur.

A similar effect can be seen in many foods and drinks; some have to be stored for several years before their true value can be appreciated. Wine is a prime example of this, the value of some bottles appreciates according to the number of years they have been allowed to stand. Dried bonito is very much the same. If you want to eat the fish itself, then of course it is best fresh, but fresh fish is no good for the dried version. First the fish is dried, then it is left to allow mold to grow. This mold greatly adds to the taste, so it has to be left for a long time in order for it to reach its final flavor. There are things that have been stored for a certain period of time which suddenly one day change into something else entirely.

To take another example, there are two kinds of students who do well in school exams. One type reads the textbooks from cover to cover, from preface to postscript without missing a single word. The other type simply picks out important points and memorizes them, knowing which sections of the book are likely to appear in the test, and gives the other parts only a cursory glance. In the short term, the latter technique is effective, allowing the student to take in the main points in a very short time. On the other hand, for those who go over their work numerous times to deepen their understanding, it will take a long time before their studies yield results. But after several years of underground effort they will achieve remarkable results, because they have become used to thinking deeply.

This type of person, one who makes underground effort over a period of time to achieve an ambition, is not necessarily very clever. If they were to stop partway through and look at what they had achieved, they might think they were slow learners with no potential to do well. If they were to stop halfway through, they would not achieve anything, so they must never give up. If they do not give up, although they may still be underwater, eventually they will break through the surface. What makes them keep going is willpower; they need to keep telling themselves that they are not permanently submerged, and when they eventually surface, they will find that they have advanced a long way toward their goal.

This is true of education in general. Of those who have children in school, there are parents who look at their children's short-term scholastic record in primary or junior high school and conclude whether or not their children are doing well. However, there is something they need to know. If the children concentrate only on the main points of their lessons and quickly go on to study ahead of time what is going to be taught the following term, they will often get good marks. This type of child, however, is not necessarily going to be successful in life.

Children who study ahead of the rest of their class are soon able to grasp what the teacher says and answer any questions put to them. At first glance, they appear to be very intelligent, but in a way they can be likened to people who do all their shopping with a credit card. They do not have any cash, so they charge everything up to their card, and pay off their debts when they receive their wages or bonus. They buy all kinds of things but are always in debt.

It is true that people who get information ahead of time will do well in the short term. In the same way, those who choose the main points of a lesson and study only these will get good marks if what they have studied appears in the test. These are common strategies and actually these people often get to savor the fruits of success. However, what I want to stress is that it is not certain that they possess real strength that will help them in their lives.

If they are blessed with a good partner and working environment, they will do well; they will succeed in their career. However, the outcome is very variable, depending on the combination of their partner and their environment, so to a great extent, their success depends on luck. On the other hand, there are others whose success does not depend on luck. No matter what kind of environment they find themselves in, no matter who they have to work with, they are able to produce consistent results. This is due to the cumulative effect I spoke of earlier.

Of the knowledge you have accumulated, there may be some which is not strictly necessary for life; this can be referred to as "unnecessary necessity."[1] In the same way, there is information taught at school that does not appear in

---

1. Refer to *An Unshakable Mind* by Ryuho Okawa (Lantern Books, 2003), p.25.

exams. However, someone who has steadfastly studied everything will be able to exhibit the same effectiveness, no matter what the situation he or she is faced with. This is the kind of person who will gradually develop great stature.

To sum up, you should not try simply to pick up the gist of a subject. In the short term, it may seem to provide a quick route to success but in the long term, it will not necessarily lead you to true victory.

9. Prepare for the Next Step, Instead of Waiting on Luck

This is equally true in business. If you are involved with retail, you will know that it is relatively simple to achieve a short-term profit. For instance, you can sell something no one else does, offer free gifts or bring out a new product. There are a number of ways to make a profit in a short time.

A product might become very popular for a limited period, but in the long term this popularity will not last. A high-selling product is capable of earning a lot of money in a very short time, but this kind of business always attracts rivals. There will be people who copy your business and as more rivals appear, business will gradually taper off. It might be good for a while, but as more competitors come into the market, your profits will go down.

Let us say you build a hotel in the center of town. In the hotel business, if the working ratio, i.e. the number of rooms that are filled, exceeds eighty percent, rival companies will move into the market. If you manage to fill more than eighty percent of your rooms, it means that there is a demand and other hotel chains will open their own establishments nearby. As a result, although you may have been very busy, as soon as a new hotel opens nearby, you will find that business suddenly drops off. On the other hand, if less than seventy percent of the rooms are filled, the operation will not be profitable. If you fill less than seventy percent of your rooms, you will be in the red, whereas if you fill more than eighty percent, you will attract rivals. So you have to try and keep the number of guests somewhere between seventy and eighty percent of capacity.

Suppose you find a good site where there are no other hotels and think to yourself, "This is a good location. If I were to build here I would be sure to make a profit." You go ahead with the project and true to your initial forecast, you make a lot of money. However, while you are busy congratulating yourself, a rival moves in and takes away your customers. If you are relying solely on the novelty value to make a profit, your business will not last; it will soon go into decline.

It is good to try to launch new businesses that no one else has tried, but when you reach a certain level of success, there is something you need to bear in mind. In the case of hotel management, it is important to ensure that the same guests keep coming back. You must provide services and facilities that will make the people who have stayed once want to come back again and again. You should not want them to return just because there are no other hotels in the neighborhood. Even if you are able to make a big profit in this way, the number of guests will gradually decrease. It is vital that you offer the kind of service that will induce them to return.

If there are no other hotels in the neighborhood, you will be able to fill eighty or ninety percent of your rooms whether you offer good service or not, but eventually a competitor will appear and your true potential will be revealed. If the competitor offers better service, you will find that they take all your customers and you will soon go out of business.

Sometimes events happen that at first glance appear to be most propitious, convenient or the answer to your prayers. Actually, they happen more often than you may think, but you should not depend on them. When these things do happen, it is quite all right for you to accept them, but when you do, you must start preparing for the next step. No matter whether the environment is good or bad, the economy buoyant or depressed, as the base you need to have an attitude of trying to offer a good product or service which will allow you to maintain a steady batting average. This may sound a little dull, but it is a very important attitude that I hope you will apply.

10. When Conditions Are Favorable,
   Sow the Seeds of Love

So far, I have concentrated on adversity, but the good times are also important. When things are going well and everything succeeds in exactly the way you had hoped, you will probably feel that invincible thinking is no longer necessary. You may think to yourself, "Everything is going according to plan, everything is working out—I have no further problems," but this is when you need to look out for hidden pitfalls.

The good times and bad times should be regarded in the following way: Hardship is a time when you are presented with many opportunities to look carefully at yourself. You have an awful lot of time to think about yourself, you become introspective and you are able to look deeply into your own character. Times of hardship are times of training.

So what should you do when things are going well? The good times are when you should practice giving love. You should not be concerned solely with benefiting yourself. Instead, make an investment in the spiritual sense, an investment in the Laws of Truth. In other words, you must give love to others.

I am not talking about profit or loss, but the more seeds of love you sow in the good times, the easier your life will be when you are faced with adversity. When things are going badly, whether or not people offer to help you will depend on how many seeds of love you were able to sow when you were doing well. To put it simply, when you are in trouble, do not stint on strengthening yourself and when times are good, sow the seeds of love; tell yourself this is the time you must practice the love that gives. This sounds like a very simple philosophy but it is, in fact, the way to sustained success.

However, when faced with adversity, people tend to crave what they do not have. They bemoan their bad luck or misfortune, and try to rely on others to help them. When things improve, they become filled with pride and believe that their success was achieved entirely through their own efforts. They become arrogant and their friends give up on them. This kind of person does all right when things are running smoothly, but as soon as the going gets tough, they collapse and find there is no one around to help.

When you look back over your past, have there been times when no one offered you advice until you were faced with some danger or crisis? If you have had this kind of experience, it is probably because you were too proud while things were going well. People who become too proud and obsessed with themselves, who think it only their due to be loved by others and to be the center of attention, will find that no one offers them advice until they have experienced a bitter failure. They are like clowns standing alone beneath the spotlight. They believed they were popular, but when they pause and look around, they find that no one else has stayed to watch. When they are in trouble and find themselves unable to cope, they finally start to ask themselves where they went wrong.

On the other hand, people who did not forget others when they were doing well and continued to sow the seeds of love, will find that when they are in trouble, someone will appear to offer advice and rescue them. There are no exceptions to this. Someone with a loving heart who shows interest in others gives hope to many and, at the same time, develops integrity. If things turn bad, this integrity will have the effect of summoning others to offer help in that person's time of need. This is always the case so please, never forget this.

People who are easily carried away with their own success should be particularly careful. Watch that you do not lose control or become too easily satisfied by simple success.

11. Aim for a Goal One Step Higher

Another type I would like to discuss here is the people who, having achieved eighty percent of a success, suddenly lose their way and end up failing. It is as if they have climbed eighty percent of a high mountain and, seeing the summit close at hand, then slip and fall. I am sure this will strike a chord in many of you who are reading this book.

Have you ever experienced anything like this? You had a little further to go before you would have achieved success but then something happened that brought your dreams to nothing. If you do not learn how to overcome this tendency, you will never achieve real success.

People who find that they are capable of reaching a certain point only to discover that success eludes them often have a subconscious fear of achievement. I would like these people to contemplate deeply. When faced with the prospect of success, they become scared and begin to sow the seeds of their own downfall. They do this because they are terrified of total success; they feel that they have not earned it and they become anxious. As a result, they always do something that causes success to slip through their fingers. When they have only a little further to go, things come to a crunch and something happens to dash their dreams. However, the problem lies in their will to succeed; they themselves are scared of achieving a one hundred percent success.

People may wish their spouse to succeed in a company and earn more. They may want their spouse to become an executive but this would make them an executive's partner; this scares them so much that they do something to ruin their partner's reputation. For instance, they may do something that causes rumors to spread. They feel that if their spouse were to become important, they themselves would not get on so well, things would become more difficult for them. As a result, they unconsciously do something to stop their partner from getting ahead. This is quite a common occurrence.

The cause of this is the fact that they have not had enough experience of real success. People who have never experienced success become scared when they realize that they might become very successful. They worry about what would happen if they were to fail, and try to escape.

When they find themselves in this kind of situation, they should tell themselves that the mountain they are facing at that moment is not Mt. Fuji, it is merely one of the foothills leading to another higher mountain—they have only reached a rest area in the mountain pass.

People like this always get into trouble when they think they can see their goal, so as they approach it, they need to set their sights on a goal that is even higher. It is important to make a habit of always thinking one step ahead, always having some further goal in sight. They must tell themselves that there is always a higher mountain waiting to be tackled. Those who are able to do this will find they never fail. They may suffer minor setbacks, but in the long run they will succeed.

To go back to the example of exams, there are those who are so relieved when they have finished an exam that they rush out to let off steam, without worrying whether or not they have passed. This kind of person will often be confronted by failure. On the other hand, there are those who, as soon as they have finished, settle straight back into studies to prepare themselves for the next test. This type of person does not easily find themselves in trouble, whereas the ones who are filled with exuberance as soon as an exam is over will find their lives a succession of ups and downs. So, when you have achieved something, I want you always to set your next goal to brace yourself, and consider how to go about steadily attaining it.

12. Think Flexibly and Turn Difficulty to Your Advantage

Another point I would like to make about invincible thinking is that in many ways, this philosophy is similar to the principles of judo. It is not sufficient to use only your own power to force your opponent to the ground. As I explained with the example of bamboo, you should make the use of troubles and difficulties, turn them to your own advantage and produce something positive from them. This is what is meant by invincible thinking.

Alone, you can only achieve a little, but if you turn some of the external forces to your advantage, you can create something much better. This is very important, so I hope you do not misunderstand this point.

Like judo, invincible thinking allows you to utilize your opponent's strength against him. When you are beset by problems and difficulties, it is not sufficient simply to endure them; you must utilize your opponent's strength to come out on top. Be flexible and think of ways to turn the situation to your advantage. If you are always thinking like this, you will find that things are constantly getting better.

Always be ready to make your next move. Ask yourself what the problem that you are now facing is and once you have identified it, work out how to get around it. If you stay several steps ahead, you will find that the outcome will always be positive.

13. Toward a Life of Daily Success

In *The Starting Point of Happiness*, I have written about the "snowball effect"[2] which is the same idea I am talking about here. If something turns out to your advantage, of course you should make use of it, but even if it does not, you should reflect upon it, learn a lesson, and use it to plant the seeds of greater progress. Whatever happens, use it to build up your store of experience, like a snowball. If you do, you will find not only will your life be more enjoyable but you will also be able to move from victory to victory.

At the moment, you are looking at life from a viewpoint that differs from positive thinking, but ultimately the result is the same. Positive thinking states that there is essentially no such thing as worry, and no such thing as evil, and this perspective leads to the monism of Light, the idea that only light exists. However, if you understand that the purpose of life in the phenomenal world is to find a brilliant light in all your experiences, nothing but success remains each day. The final result is exactly the same as the result of positive thinking.

If positive thinking is taken to mean you can instantly attain a high level of awareness, although this philosophy

2. Refer to *The Starting Point of Happiness* by Ryuho Okawa (Lantern Books, 2001), pp.78–80.

may allow you to get ahead, your growth will be only superficial. When you are faced with various ordeals on a daily basis, it is important that you use these to build up the "muscle" of your soul and add to its true strength.

If you succeed in doing this, you will actually find that you have developed quite a strong unshakable mind. One aspect of invincible thinking is that the unshakable mind is greatly fortified. It is impervious to hardship. When you are confronted by problems, it will take them in, and convert them into nourishment for the soul. When you practice invincible thinking, it is as if you are looking around, ready to face any troubles or difficulties, and as soon as something happens you absorb it and convert it into strength. This philosophy is very powerful and it is the manifestation of unshakable mind.

If someone compliments you, express your appreciation and tell yourself that it is because you had the help of numerous people that you were able to do well. Do not think of achievement as your own, but remain humble; think of success as being the result of the help of God and numerous other people. The more you achieve, the more humble you should be. On the other hand, when you are faced with hardship, think of it as nourishment to help you grow and bear fruit. If you think in this way, you need not fear any adversity. When difficulty comes, you can accept it willingly, as a time when you can learn lessons. Accepting adversity in this way, you will gain strength to allow your soul to grow and give out a new light.

When adversity comes, for instance if you are demoted, take a drop in salary, or you are working for a company that goes bankrupt, you will become introspective, so use this time to your fullest advantage. In other words, at a time like this when you become contemplative and reflective, you should take this opportunity to temper your soul. When things finally get better, then you can make an effort to move in a positive direction and produce results.

Another way of putting this would be to say that you should make use of both the philosophy of self-reflection of the Buddha and the philosophy of positivity of Hermes.[3] When things are going badly, focus on self-reflection as taught by Shakyamumi Buddha, and when things are going well, aim to achieve further progress and development as taught by Hermes. My teachings include both ideas—self-reflection and progress—and you can always succeed by using both effectively.

Aim to grow and develop every year. After suffering through adversity, it is not enough to practice self-reflection and manage to allow the plus and minus to cancel each other out. Instead, face the storms that approach and take their strength for yourself. Do not be satisfied merely to weather a storm until it dies down, then come up the same as you were before. Rather, absorb all of what you

---

3. Hermes, a part of the Buddha consciousness, is the god of prosperity and
    art. He lived in ancient Greece and preached the Laws of Prosperity rich
    with artistic values. Refer to *The Golden Laws* by Ryuho Okawa (Lantern
    Books, 2002), pp.151–153.

have experienced while confronting difficulties and transform it into energy within you. If you look back at the way you were one year, two years, three years ago, you must be able to say that you have definitely come a long way, and that you have grown in stature. I would like you sometimes to check that this is true for you.

If you continually grow like the bamboo, you are achieving success in your life on a daily basis. I would like to finish this book with the following advice: Make use of both the philosophies of self-reflection and progress to make yourself invincible.

Postscript

This book is based on four weekday seminars held in June and July in 1989 for members of Happy Science. My intention was to demonstrate how to win in daily life by providing numerous examples from many different perspectives. It is a book that can be read in a variety of ways, offering ideas on success, life, happiness and the methodology of enlightenment.

If you read this book carefully, I am sure you will realize that at the core of this philosophy bridging self-reflection and progress, lies a deep insight into life, and a wisdom born of experience.

This book makes clear the essence of my teachings and is essential reading for anyone seeking success.

Ryuho Okawa
President
Happy Science

ABOUT THE AUTHOR

Ryuho Okawa, founder of Happy Science, Kofuku-no-Kagaku in Japan, has devoted his life to the exploration of the Truth and ways to happiness.

He was born in 1956 in Tokushima, Japan. He graduated from the University of Tokyo. In March 1981, he received his higher calling and awakened to the hidden part of his consciousness, El Cantare. After working at a major Tokyo-based trading house and studying international finance at the Graduate Center of the City University of New York, he established Happy Science in 1986.

Since then, he has been designing spiritual workshops for people from all walks of life, from teenagers to business executives. He is known for his wisdom, compassion and commitment to educating people to think and act in spiritual and religious ways.

He has published over 500 books, including *The Laws of the Sun, The Golden Laws, The Laws of Eternity, The Science of Happiness,* and *The Essence of Buddha.* His books have sold millions of copies worldwide. He has also produced successful feature-length films (including animations) based on his works.

The members of Happy Science follow the path he teaches, ministering to people who need help by sharing his teachings.

LANTERN BOOKS BY RYUHO OKAWA

The Laws of the Sun: *Discover the Origin of Your Soul*
978-1-930051-62-1

The Golden Laws: *History through the Eyes of the Eternal Buddha*
978-1-930051-61-4

The Laws of Eternity: *Unfolding the Secrets of the Multidimensional Universe*
978-1-930051-63-8

The Starting Point of Happiness
A Practical and Intuitive Guide to Discovering Love, Wisdom, and Faith
978-1-930051-18-8

Love, Nurture, and Forgive: *A Handbook to Add a New Richness to Your Life*
978-1-930051-78-2

An Unshakable Mind: *How to Overcome Life's Difficulties*
978-1-930051-77-5

The Origin of Love: *On the Beauty of Compassion*
978-1-59056-052-5

Invincible Thinking: *There Is No Such Thing As Defeat*
978-1-59056-051-8

Guideposts to Happiness: *Prescriptions for a Wonderful Life*
978-1-59056-056-3

The Philosophy of Progress: *Higher Thinking for Developing Infinite Prosperity*
978-1-59056-057-0

The Laws of Happiness: *The Four Principles for a Successful Life*
978-1-59056-073-0

Ten Principles of Universal Wisdom
The Truth of Happiness, Enlightenment, and the Creation of an Ideal World
978-1-59056-094-5

Tips to Find Happiness
Creating a Harmonious Home for Your Spouse, Your Children, and Yourself
978-1-59056-080-8

Order at www.lanternbooks.com

What is Happy Science?

Happy Science is an organization of people who aim to cultivate their souls and deepen their love and wisdom through learning and practicing the teachings (the Truth) of Ryuho Okawa. Happy Science spreads the light of Truth, with the aim of creating an ideal world on Earth.

Members learn the Truth through books, lectures, and seminars to acquire knowledge of a spiritual view of life and the world. They also practice meditation and self-reflection daily, based on the Truth they have learned. This is the way to develop a deeper understanding of life and build characters worthy of being leaders in society who can contribute to the development of the world.

Events and Seminars

There are regular events and seminars held at your local temple. These include practicing meditation, watching video lectures, study group sessions, seminars and book events. All these offer a great opportunity to meet like-minded friends on the same path to happiness and for further soul development. By being an active participant at your local temples you will be able to:

- Know the purpose and meaning of life
- Know the true meaning of love and create better relationships
- Learn how to meditate to achieve serenity of mind
- Learn how to overcome life's challenges

...and much more

International Seminars

International seminars are held in Japan each year where members have a chance to deepen their enlightenment and meet friends from all over the world who are studying Happy Science's teachings.

Happy Science Monthly Publications

Happy Science has been publishing monthly magazines for English readers around the world since 1994. Each issue contains Master Okawa's latest lectures, words of wisdom, stories of remarkable life-changing experiences, up-to-date news from around the globe, in-depth explanations of the different aspects of Happy Science, movie and book reviews, and much more to guide readers to a happier life.

Hundreds of interesting back-issues of our Monthly publications are available at your nearest temple.

You can pick up the latest issue from your nearest temple or subscribe to have them delivered *(please contact your nearest temple from the contacts page)*. Happy Science Monthly is available in many other languages too, including Portuguese, Spanish, French, German, Chinese, and Korean.

Our Welcome e-Booklet

You can read our Happy Science Welcome Introductory Booklet and find out the basics of Happy Science, testimonies from members and even register with us:

http://content.yudu.com/Library/A1e44v/HappyScienceIntro

If you have any questions, please email us at:
inquiry@happy-science.org

CONTACTS

Find more information about locations, activities, and events offered at Happy Science by visiting the websites below

Japan
www.kofuku-no-kagaku.or.jp/en
Tokyo
1-6-7 Togoshi, Shinagawa,
Tokyo,
142-0041 Japan
Tel: 81-3-6384-5770
Fax: 81-3-6384-5776
tokyo@happy-science.org

United States of America
New York
www.happyscience-ny.org
79 Franklin Street, New York,
New York 10013, U.S.A.
Tel: 1-212-343-7972
Fax: 1-212-343-7973
ny@happy-science.org

Los Angeles
www.happyscience-la.org
1590 E. Del Mar Blvd.,
Pasadena, CA 91106, U.S.A.
Tel: 1-626-395-7775
Fax: 1-626-395-7776
la@happy-science.org

San Francisco
www.happyscience-sf.org
525 Clinton St., Redwood City,
CA 94062, U.S.A
Tel: 1-650-363-2777
Fax: same
sf@happy-science.org

New York East
nyeast@happy-science.org

New Jersey
newjersey@happyscience.org

Florida
www.happyscience-fl.org
florida@happy-science.org

Chicago
chicago@happy-science.org

Boston
boston@happy-science.org

Atlanta
atlanta@happy-science.org

Albuquerque
abq@happy-science.org

Hawaii
www.happyscience-hi.org
hi@happy-science.org

Kauai
kauai-hi@happy-science.org

Canada
Toronto
http://www.happy-science.ca
toronto@happy-science.org

Vancouver
vancouver@happy-science.org

Europe
London
www.happyscience-eu.org
3 Margaret Street, London W1W
8RE, United Kingdom
Tel: 44-20-7323-9255
Fax: 44-20-7323-9344
eu@happy-science.org

Oceania
Sydney
www.happyscience.org.au
sydney@happy-science.org

Sydney East
bondi@happy-science.org

Melbourne
melbourne@happy-science.org

New Zealand
newzealand@happy-science.org

To find out more Happy Science
locations worldwide, go to
http://www.kofuku-no-
kagaku.or.jp/en/page9.html

Want to know more?

Thank you for choosing this book. If you would like to receive further information about titles by Ryuho Okawa, please send the following information either by fax, post or e-mail to your nearest Happy Science Branch.

1. Title Purchased

_____

2. Please let us know your impression of this book.

_____

3. Are you interested in receiving a catalog of Ryuho Okawa's books?

       Yes ❏   No ❏

4. Are you interested in receiving Happy Science Monthly?

       Yes ❏   No ❏

Name : Mr / Mrs / Ms / Miss : _____

Address : _____

_____

_____

Phone: _____

Email: _____

Thank you for your interest in Lantern Books.